The Good Earth
Bath, Beauty &
Health Book

Casey Kellar

Published by
Krause Publications
700 E. State St
Iola, WI 54990-0001
715-445-2214
www.krause.com

Please call or write for our free catalog of publications. Our toll-free number to place an order or obtain a free catalog is 800-258-0929 or please use our regular business telephone 715-445-2214 for editorial comment and further information.

Library of Congress Catalog Number 00-110068
ISBN 0-87341-954-5

Neither the publisher nor author can be held responsible for any injuries, losses, or other damages resulting from the use of information in this book (due to different conditions, tools, and individual skills); however, great care has been taken to ensure that the information in this book is accurate.

Mother Nature illustration by Gary Carle.

Dedication

To my customers and friends: this book is a result of your constant curiosity about compounding and questions about natural ingredients. It is for those of you who want to play in your kitchens and make pampering products or home remedies that are fun to use and cost effective. It is you who keeps prodding me to create and produce, and I thank you.

Special thank yous to:

My husband Byron for always supporting me in all that I do.

Seiche Sanders for finding me, following through, and putting this all together.

Amy Tincher-Durik and the staff at Krause for all of their hard work on this book.

Why I Wrote This Book...

Let's take a journey together. Travel with me to your own special spa and health retreat, where you have control of your comfort, pampering, and personal pleasures. This is a place where you control the cost and safety of these treatments, knowing that they are free of harsh, irritating chemicals or additives, and you understand and control the natural ingredients used.

See yourself emerging from this place not only relaxed, but also comforted and in radiant beauty with clear eyes, glossy hair, glowing skin, and with money still in your checkbook…

About now, you're probably saying to yourself, "Wait! I've never heard of this place before…"

Well, then, follow me through this book, and I will show you how to make safe and effective bath and spa treatments and home remedies that are natural—and fun and simple to make—at a fraction of the price you would pay if you went to the store or spa/salon to get them.

If you feel overworked, stressed, and fatigued…

If you don't want to pay an arm and a leg for quality pampering and self-help remedies…

If you want only safe, natural formulas and environmentally sound products…

You are the reason I wrote this book. I am going to show you how to make Mother Nature your Fairy Godmother. I have devised natural, simple, and fun formulas that will help you overcome some of today's barriers to enjoying your well being, along with natural formulas that will produce spa-quality beauty results.

Having control of your toiletries and remedies, along with taking some time for yourself, will help you feel better and cope with everyday challenges. When you take these first few steps to care for and pamper yourself, it is my hope that you will start on a journey to self-discovery and finding your needs. Take a few moments to listen to what your body is telling you. In this busy "run from one thing to another" world, it is all too easy to forget about self-nurturing. And as the saying goes, "How can you be effective and take care of others when you don't take time to take care of yourself?" If you are troubled by tension and fatigue, and feel like you never get a moment to yourself, gather a few ingredients, close the door to the world, and take some time to pamper yourself. You may not think you have time, but that is the time when you need that special treatment the most. Then you can go back—refreshed— into the "jungle" and get everything you need to do done, more efficiently and calmer than you would have had you not taken those few minutes for yourself.

Nature intends for us to use our senses and live in balance. Use this book to help you gain balance by spending a little "good-health" pampering time. You can do this in a few quiet moments alone, by sharing the time with a special friend and making the formulas I have given you in this book, or by simply sharing formulas you have made with a friend.

Enjoy!

Table of Contents

Introduction

*H*ey, Cinderella, here's how to make Mother Nature your Fairy Godmother…

Are you always shopping with concerns of being environmentally and politically correct? Wondering if the product you are purchasing is tested on animals? Wondering if it is a good value? Is the product made from the best natural ingredients? Well, Cinderella, now you can take charge!

For most people, a homemade item is the best, because the ingredients that go into it are familiar and safe, and a loving touch has been applied. It is the very thought that this item was either created just for you or handmade by a caring person for your benefit. Perhaps it's the thought that the item you make yourself is the ultimate token of self-care and pampering. Not only will you have the satisfaction of creating your own products, gifts, and "traditions" in your kitchen, but you will also save a great deal of money by making and packaging them yourself.

There is even a measure of convenience when you make products yourself, from scratch, the convenience of only making what you need, in the quantity you need, when you need it, which means less waste. This is particularly true when you consider that you will not be using preservatives or synthetic product "extenders" in your homemade products. All of this takes a little planning and organization, but the formulas are quick and easy, and you can be oh-so creative with the packaging!

Just think of the surprise and elation of loved ones and friends when they receive a care package made by you. You can take care of your own needs as well—and not worry about what's on the label, because you already know! You know it has not been animal-tested and is safe to use. You will find that "traditions" you have only heard about and thought were lost will revive. Do you remember seeing the old story on TV about an ailing child, and grandma makes "her special sore throat elixir" to help the child through the misery of a cold? Well, you just might become famous in your own family circle for your helpful and healthful elixirs and potions made with love (at a fraction of the cost of store-bought). You can also play Cinderella for yourself or others by making spa-quality treatments at home (which are also far more economical).

By correlating centuries-old beauty and health secrets with up-to-date technology, this book offers safe, easy, quality, and economical formula options for beauty, self-pampering, and good health. You will be using and nurturing Mother Nature's gifts to make the most of all your homemade products.

The Life and Times of Nature ...

How We Got Started

"As old as the hills," the saying goes, and indeed the hills do talk to us. As far back as recorded time, which were hieroglyphics scratched on walls, is evidence of early peoples using herbs, clays, and berries to both heal and paint their bodies.

Many of today's drugs were derived from years of observance of human usage and experimentation. In the days before our concerns about animal testing, we were testing on ourselves through early alchemy. Many of the poor, unfortunate women thought to be witches who were burned at the stake through the years were the early healers, herbalists, and lotion and potion makers. Now, thank goodness, we can practice giving our families and ourselves comfort with herbal remedies and potions for good health and beauty and not risk trial by fire!

It is believed that our early ancestors observed animal behavior; when an animal was ill, it would eat certain plants that were not in its usual diet. As a result of these observations, people then would sample these plants and notice various effects. These herbs and plants were then used by early shamans and "witch doctors," who incorporated them into their practice.

Through the years, cures and treatments turned interests to sanitation and prevention, and then to personal improvement in the form of beautification. The earliest beautification was with warriors: berries and clays were made into body paints that were used in ceremonies to help "psyche" the warriors into hunting bravery or combat. Paints were not only used for ceremonial purposes to help the warrior mentally prepare for an ordeal; they could also serve for looking fiercer to the opponent to strike fear into his heart.

Herbs were made into smells, too: early "smudge sticks" still used by many Native Americans were used to purify, cleanse, and fragrance ceremonies and cleansing rooms.

Through the years, women found power in healing, nurturing, and using their own beauty for personal gain. The Romans were famous for their bathhouses, and Cleopatra was making lipstick and rouges from berries and soaking in flowers to make her beauty even more appealing. And, in the Victorian Era, the corner drug store sold lots of herbal tinctures and floral waters, glycerin, witch hazel, and other items that Victorian ladies would buy and make into beauty treatments and home remedies.

As you can see, in every country and from every race, there are similarities of early health and beauty rituals that have been recorded and used through the years to get us where we are today. The big difference today that has raised our concerns is the abundance of engineered, synthetic chemicals that replace our dwindling natural resources as demand grows.

THE WORD "DRUG" IS ACTUALLY LINKED TO THE EARLY GERMAN WORD *DROGE*, MEANING TO DRY, AS IN DRYING HERBS, CLAYS, AND BERRIES, WHICH IS THE FIRST STEP IN PROCESSING HERBS INTO MEDICINES. ASPIRIN WAS FIRST MADE FROM WHITE WILLOW BARK AND MEADOWSWEET (MEADOWSWEET IS AN OLD SCIENTIFIC NAME FOR *SPIREA*, WHICH EVOLVED INTO "SPIRIN" IN THE WORD ASPIRIN).

When you are dependent on a commodities market and supply and demand, prices fluctuate so much that for most manufacturers, it is cheaper to "reproduce" natural products from petrol and other bases, most of which just serve to cheapen the product and give us cause for concern (and long names we cannot understand), instead of using the real thing. Because of this, we have seen a real resurgence of "natural base products" being introduced. Day spa and salons are using herb, clay, aromatherapy, and mineral treatments that promise natural ingredients and wonderful results.

With this book, you can do much of this for yourself. Many of the formulas will need to be made fresh or kept in the refrigerator, but the effects will be great, at a fraction of the cost, and you will be making them with your own hands, with love and control of the ingredients, much like our ancestors.

Mother Nature Says ...

UNLESS OTHERWISE NOTED, ALL OF THE FORMULAS IN THIS BOOK SHOULD BE STORED IN A COVERED CONTAINER IN A COOL, DARK PLACE.

INGREDIENTS AND EQUIPMENT

You can find most of the ingredients used in the formulas at health food stores, pharmacies or drug stores, or grocery stores. If you live in a small town with few resources, you may need to ask a store to order an ingredient especially for you, or look to the Internet or mail-order companies. I have included a list of some of the more uncommon ingredients used in this book, each with a brief description (see page 109).

You will be using a number of common household items as equipment, but please note that it is always best to use stainless steel bowls and mixing tools. Plastic often picks up the fragrance of the herb extracts or essential oil you are using, so if you use plastic, it should not be used again for anything else. Some metals can have a slight chemical reaction to certain herbs or essentials, but stainless steel will always clean up totally in very hot water and will not retain any residue/odor from previous projects, nor will it react to herbal extracts or essential oils.

Helpful Items to Have

Cutting board

Decorative or unusual jars, bottles, tins

Double boiler

Eyedroppers (glass is best if you are going to reuse)

Food processor

Kitchen scale

Knife

Grater

Mortar and pestle

Peeler

Shakers

Sifter

Stainless steel measuring spoons

Stainless steel mixing utensils (not plastic or wood)

Stainless steel or glass measuring cups

Stainless steel or glass mixing bowls

You may also want to accumulate scraps of lace, ribbon, fabric, silk flowers, silk fruit, and so forth for decorating your lotions, potions, and herbal remedies for gift giving. It is also nice to have some "Handmade by" labels to put on your products. You can find them in specialty cooking stores or you could also make them on your computer.

Mother Nature Says ...

EACH FORMULA INCLUDES INFORMATION ABOUT ITS SHELF LIFE. REMEMBER TO LABEL YOUR CREATIONS SO YOU KNOW WHEN THE SHELF LIFE HAS EXPIRED!

The Good Earth Bath, Beauty & Health Book

CHAPTER 1

Aromatherapy and Herbal Therapy

In This Chapter:

Casey's Favorite Carrier Oil Formula

Making Essential Oil

Infusions

Extracts

Basic Syrup Formula

Decoction

Tincture

Compress

Poultice

Ointment/Salve

Steam Inhalant

Skin Washes/Sprays

Herbal therapy and aromatherapy have some synergies, in that they both affect the mental and physical well being of humans; however, one is absorbed through the nasal cavity and the lungs, and sometimes through skin application for its effectiveness (aromatherapy), and the other through oral ingestion and absorption into the body's chemistry or through skin application (herbal therapy). In this chapter, we will talk about some common herbs and uses for herbal home remedies, toiletries, and beauty applications, as well as some of the most commonly used aromatherapy oils and their observed responses. I will also teach you the basics on how to make essential oils, an infusion, a tincture, and an ointment/salve.

All fragrance mediums were originally made from organic materials. Through the years, technology developed, and now many of the fragrances we buy are made from totally synthetic or "nature identical" artificial ingredients. When making something in this book and using a commercially prepared essential oil, make sure it is a naturally derived product. The less alcohol and other fillers added the better, because these will dilute the potency of the actual essential used in the formula and make it less effective. There are many good-quality essential oils currently available; you just need to make sure of what you are buying, or you can make your own essential oil at home.

CASEY'S FAVORITE CARRIER OIL FORMULA

My favorite carrier oils for making essential oils are apricot kernel oil and jojoba oil. Apricot kernel oil has good stability, is cost effective, and is a great lubricant to help the essence of the flowers or plant material "release" into the carrier. Jojoba oil has natural Vitamin E in it so it is not only a quality oil, but it also has a little better shelf life than apricot kernel oil. The downside to jojoba is that it lacks some of the lighter lube effects that aid the absorption of the flowers and plant materials into the oil (it will happen, it just takes a little longer). Plus, jojoba oil is much more expensive.

Here is a simple solution to get the best of my favorite carriers. With a 50/50 blend of the two oils, you will get a pretty fair release time of the flowers and plant materials into the blend (some of jojoba's natural preserving qualities, and a more cost-effective carrier oil).

Knowing that you have my favorite carrier oil formula, there are several other possibilities to change the cost. Rather than give you 2 cups of this here and 1 cup of that there kind of formula, I would rather "teach you to fish" by way of totally explaining how this works so you can adjust the formula as you go, because you will want to use various flowers, herbs, plant materials, and citrus items. Here is how you make an essential oil:

MAKING ESSENTIAL OIL

We will be extracting the "essence" of flowers, herbs, citrus, or spices by soaking a large amount of the property you are extract-

ing in a small amount of natural oil. I will explain the process to you and give you a sample formula. Once you understand the process, you will be able to make many kinds of essential oils. This is a home formula, and even though it will be potent, some commercial ways of using distillation in the process will make a commercial product stronger than your home-based one. Remember to adjust the amounts of essential oil used (I have written the formulas in this book around commercial grade, because most people will buy their essential oils rather than make them), so if you are using your own oil made with this formula, make sure to increase the amount used in it.

As was stated on the previous page, always start with a quality carrier oil with the best stability (natural shelf life) and the least odor of its own. Cooking oils just won't do. Now, here is your lesson:

You Will Need

3-4 cups of flower petals (or herbs, spices, or citrus peels)
1 cup carrier oil (you may not use all of it)

You always want to use the least amount of carrier oil you can get away with, because you want the essence to break down and be as concentrated as possible, so go light on the carrier oil (remember the carrier oil is a 50/50 blend of jojoba and apricot kernel oil, or your variation thereof).

Flower petals, like roses, are light and fluffy; I would measure approximately 1/8 to 1/4 the size of the flower's mass to the amount of oil mass. Okay, okay so I'll break down and give you one exact formula for this, but I really want you to get a feel for this so you can make other essential oils for yourself …

You Will Need

3 cups flower petals
1/2 cup carrier oil (approximately)

Before you add these two together in your jar or container, using either your hands (wear plastic gloves) or a mortar and pestle, lightly "bruise" the material you will be extracting from. You do this because it will open up the fibers and start the "bleeding" of the plant material into the oil. Now, grab your processing jar or container, and put the flowers in, then pour the oil over the top. Put the lid on and shake vigorously for 1 to 2 minutes, and the process has started. The next thing you will need is a dark place (inside your home) in which to store it and some patience. Let it mature about a month (take it out and shake it vigorously at least once a week). Then, strain the mixture with a fine strainer or cheesecloth and discard everything except the clear essential oil that you have made. Store the oil in amber or dark glass vials or bottles. The shelf life is 12 to 18 months, if it is stored in a cool, dark place.

Repeat this process with herbs and spices. Most essential oils are single note (one herb or flower), but in the old days, many tinctures (see page 18) were made from two or more items; you could try making "essential" quality perfume oils this way as well, and then just dilute them with a little more carrier oil later to give as body perfumes.

Here are some rules to remember about making essential oils:

1. Don't eat it! Even though it is natural, this method of extracting the plant "essence" is meant for the purpose of fragrancing or using in personal care items, not for eating.
2. Always start with fresh ingredients. Old, dried items don't have the "life" needed for

making essential oils. Basically, what happens during this process is as the flowers, herbs, etc. "rot" and disintegrate into the oil, they leave their "essence" in the form of moisture in the small amount of carrier oil; this essence, or liquid, is drawn out and preserved in the oil as the body (bulk or fiber) of the flower or plant disintegrates.

3. Do not use items treated with pesticides or that have not been hand selected and hand cleaned by you. Always remove excess water (air dry first if necessary).

4. Use "meaty" materials—flowers and plant materials that have a lot of fiber to them and are not almost all water content. For example, even though we would not use lettuce to make an essential oil, think about how much water content there is in lettuce. Because water and oil don't mix, and there is very little to it other than water, you could not extract any natural oils, flavor, or fragrance from it.

Most herbs work great because they are fibrous and aromatic, as are citrus peels and most spices. Choose your flowers wisely. If there is enough fiber to them and they are aromatic, this method will work (see the following page for a listing of flowers, herbs, spices, and citrus that work well).

INFUSIONS, EXTRACTS, AND TINCTURES

The main difference between infusions, extracts, and tinctures is that infusions are made with hot water, while extracts and tinctures are made with alcohol.

Infusions can be made with fresh or dried ingredients. When you make tea, you are really making an infusion. It is as simple as pouring hot water over plant materials. The stronger you want the infusion, the more plant material to water ratio and the longer the steeping time. This is a great way to make an infusion for use in the formulas in this book. Here is my favorite when I want to make a strong infusion:

You Will Need

1/4 cup dried herb
1 cup boiling water

Pour the boiling water over the herb and let sit for 30 minutes (cover while steeping to hold in the vapors). Put in a dark glass bottle. Drink warm.

Shelf life: 1 to 2 days

Mother Nature Says ...

WHEN MAKING A HOMEMADE TEA OR INFUSION, YOU CAN PUT THE MATERIAL (SINGLE HERB OR HERB MIX) IN A STORE-BOUGHT TEA BAG (YOU CAN PURCHASE THESE AT HEALTH FOOD STORES), OR PUT IN A TEA INFUSER.

Extracts are made by mixing dried plant materials with alcohol. If you use fresh materials to mix with alcohol, in the method described below, you will have made a **tincture.** Both are used in many herbal health and homemade natural remedies.

Look back at the basic formula I gave you for making essential oil (on page 13). Remember how I said I really wanted you to get a "feel" for this? If you substitute alcohol (use 90-proof vodka or everclear) for the carrier oil, you are now making an extract or a tincture (depending on whether you are using dried or fresh materials). Again, you want to make them as potent as possible, so use just enough alcohol to cover the plant materials and follow the same steps for processing and maturing the tincture or extract as you did for essential oil.

These are all ways of drawing out a plant's essence into a medium so that it can be used in a formula or preparation. Here is a starting list of flowers, herbs, and spices as an example of natural elements that can be prepared into any of the methods of making essential oils, infusions, extracts, or tinctures to use in personal care products or for fragrancing:

Allspice
Basil (use plant portion)
Cedar (use plant and bark portions)
Cloves
Geranium (use flowers and/or leaves)
Ginger (use sliced root)
Grapefruit (use peel)
Lavender (use flowering portion)
Lemon (use peel)
Orange (use peel)
Peppermint (use plant portion)
Rose (use petals)
Rosemary (use plant portion)
Thyme (use plant portion)
Vanilla (use bean)

Aromatherapy Uses of Some Essential Oils and How It All Works…

Aromatherapy not only evokes certain responses, but also certain memory patterns. When you smell something, it is the response of your olfactory nerve, which contains about 50 million receptors located in mucous membranes. Small hairs collect odors and convert them into messages, which are relayed through the olfactory response to the brain for processing. As this process occurs, it stirs a certain memory or feeling associated with that particular odor. This response may be conscious or unconscious and can trigger changes in body temperature, appetite, stress level, sexual arousal, mood, and feelings. Olfactory nerve cells can be regenerated and can temporarily "wear out" from a certain smell (a great example of this is when you have cooked fish, onions, or garlic, and don't smell it any more, but someone else walks in your home and says "Wow! What's that smell?" Your olfactory response has temporarily "burned out" on that smell, but someone new to the scene can smell it).

Here are common responses to some essential oils. They are "average responses" based on testing, and responses can vary, because we are all unique individuals, with our own set of memories. Put together some oils and do some smell association and observance testing on your own.

Cedarwood and juniper:	Cleansing, outdoors
Chamomile:	Calming, herbal
Clove and cinnamon:	Contemplation, kitchen memories, holidays
Eucalyptus:	Balance, well being
Frankincense and myrrh:	Meditative, musty yet animal attraction
Ginger and grapefruit:	Energizing, spicy, fresh
Jasmine:	Calming (can be used as an antidepressant)
Lavender:	Relaxing, calming
Lemon and grapefruit:	Stimulating, refreshing
Lemon and lime:	Refreshing, summer
Rose:	Aphrodisiac, slightly hypnotic
Rosemary:	Stimulating, raises spirits, outdoors
Spearmint:	Uplifting, fresh
Tea-tree oil:	Disinfecting, antiseptic medicine
Vanilla:	Relaxing (can be used as an aphrodisiac for men)

Making Remedies at Home

Using herbs to make your own remedies at home can be self-satisfying. Make sure the herbs you use are safe for consumption. This understanding of basic home formulations will help you start on a kitchen adventure of making your own soothers and potions in the same spirit of people who make their own jams and jellies.

How to Make a Syrup

To make a syrup, you can use sugar, unrefined sugar, or honey, as well as an infusion, decoction, or a tincture. If you want to use a tincture that you purchased at a health food store, the usual ratio is one part tincture to four parts water; this will give you the right amount with which to add sugar to make a syrup. Usually made into cough remedies, syrups are a great way to get kids to take herbal remedies because the "spoonful of sugar" theory still works. The sweetness also helps disguise the less pleasant tasting herbs such as valerian root (it is a great relaxation and sleep aid but smells and tastes like old socks).

Basic Syrup Formula

You Will Need

- 1 cup sugar, unrefined sugar, or honey (choose one)
- 1-1/4 cup herbal infusion (strong tea made from the herb of your choice) or decoction (see below)

Heat the infusion or decoction in a saucepan. Slowly add the sugar or honey while stirring until completely dissolved. Pour into a dark bottle and make sure to cap.

Shelf Life: 1 to 3 months (longer if you refrigerate)

How to Make a Decoction

A decoction is a more potent form of tea or infusion. This method involves a more concentrated extraction of an herb's active ingredients and is used mostly for tree bark, roots, and some highly fibrous herbs. This allows for more of a "cooking" process to release the herb into the water.

Mother Nature Says ...

It is best to use a cork when capping a bottle. Fermentation happens over time, and if you use a regular cap, you must open it from time to time to release vapors, or the bottle can explode. Corks let the contents "breathe," so combustion may not happen.

You Will Need

1 cup dried herb or root
2 cups water

Place the herbs or roots in a saucepan and add the water. Stir. Bring to a boil. Reduce to low heat, cover, and let simmer for 1 hour. As with a tea (infusion), this is good for about one to two days (three to four doses) unless you preserve it as syrup (see the previous page).

HOW TO MAKE A TINCTURE

Tinctures are alcohol and flowers or herbs combined. In this process, alcohol is used to pull the essential from the herb or flower into the alcohol solution to "suspend" the essence there to be used at a later time. Sometimes you can buy tinctures at health food stores. Tinctures are sometimes called for in formulas or used to dab on the body, depending on the application. If you want to try making one yourself, here is a formula to try. Look for everclear alcohol or use any low-odor 90-proof alcohol that you can buy at a liquor store (90-proof vodka works well).

Rosemary Tincture

4-5 medium-length, fresh rosemary stalks
3/4 cup 90-proof vodka or other clear
    low-odor 90-proof drinking alcohol

Chop the rosemary into 1/2-inch strips and gently "bruise" the plant by "hammering" gently with your fist on a wood cutting board. Put the alcohol in an amber or dark glass bottle, then stuff in the cut and bruised rosemary. Place the cap on the bottle and shake vigorously for 1 minute. Set in a cool, dark place for 6 to 8 weeks (shake for 1 minute every week). Strain the tincture from the plant pieces remaining, then store in a cool, dark place.

Shelf Life: Approx. 1 year

HOW TO MAKE A COMPRESS

A compress is an externally applied cloth or pad that is soaked in an herbal tea, decoction, or extract and water mix. It is used to help with the healing of muscle injuries, wounds, or external pain. Sometimes, a cold compress is used for headaches or muscle sprains. Cotton or gauze is the best compress material.

Make a tea or decoction and then soak the fabric to be applied in the liquid. Wring out and apply. When swelling is involved or for a headache, put in the freezer until cold and then apply. Warm compresses intermittent with cold are great for swelling because this helps relieve pressure.

For muscles, try wintergreen, camphor, and eucalyptus teas, and use lavender and chamomile to make a compress for a headache (remember to chill the compress).

HOW TO MAKE A POULTICE

This is similar to a compress, but instead of a liquid-soaked fabric, the whole herb is applied to the affected area. Boil the fresh herb or root and then strain and squeeze out any excess water. Place the herb on a thin layer of gauze and then fold the gauze over just enough to hold the herb in (it will look like a big tea bag). Apply the poultice to the affected area. Replace every 3 to 4 hours, as needed. The herb you use depends on what you want to accomplish (for instance, rosemary and chamomile are a great combination for healing and a mild antiseptic).

HOW TO MAKE AN OINTMENT/SALVE

An ointment is made from oils or fats and, unlike a crème or lotion, it does not absorb into the skin but forms a separate layer over it. The reason you would want to do this is to help the skin where it is weak or damaged or where some additional protection is needed from moisture (because of possible infection). A great example of when an ointment is good is in the case of diaper rash. You want to protect the skin from any more urine contact that would further aggravate the condition.

You Will Need

1/2 cup beeswax
1/2 cup petroleum jelly
1 tablespoon jojoba oil
5 drops herbal or flower essential oil
   (i.e. chamomile or slippery elm)

Melt the wax and petroleum jelly in a double boiler on the stove. Stir until mixed. Add the essential or herbal oil slowly after you remove from heat. Continue stirring until the mix starts to thicken. Pour into dark glass jars while still warm.

Shelf Life: 4 to 6 months

HOW TO MAKE A STEAM INHALANT

For colds, asthma, or sinusitis, place a small amount of herb, essential oil, or tincture (for example, eucalyptus) in a bowl with 1 to 2 cups of boiling water. Lean over the bowl with a towel draped over it and your head and inhale the steam vapors for at least 5 minutes. Make sure to stay warm and do not go into a cold environment for at least 1 hour after inhalation.

SKIN WASHES/SPRAYS

These are simple to make from infusions and can be used to bathe irritated skin, wounds, or sores with the appropriate herb. Use a cotton ball to apply the liquid to the affected area or use a plastic spray bottle. This is a great way to dispense arnica and tea-tree oil (arnica to help with bruising and tea-tree for a disinfectant). Then, if you desire, mix the infusion with 50 percent witch hazel, and you have a great natural first aid spray.

The Good Earth Bath, Beauty & Health Book

CHAPTER 2

Potpourri and Sachets...
Useful Fragrance Items
for Your Home

In This Chapter:

Homemade Potpourri

Foot Deodorizer Potpourri
Sachet/Ball

Potpourri Closet Freshener

All-in-one Linen and Sweater
Protector and Cedar Chest
Revitalizer

Air Freshener

Homemade Potpourri:
How It Works

Most people think you just take some dry flowers, toss them together, and—voila!—you have potpourri. Actually, it takes a couple of other components and some technique to make good potpourri.

You must start with flowers that are dried or freeze-dried. If you use fresh flowers, you will have a mold and mildew smell and you will have to toss the whole batch. Dried flower petals from roses, hydrangea, globes, lavender, marigolds, babies breath—almost every flower, pod, and leaf you can imagine—can be dried and tossed together to make a beautiful color combination to turn into potpourri. Because most flowers have little or no smell when dried, it really is more for color that you dry and blend the flowers. You are the designer: choose flowers for color, texture, and season appeal. Once you have selected your flowers and dried them thoroughly, you are ready to start.

The orris root works as a "fixative" for the fragrance in the botanicals and will really make the fragrance last. The orris root will bind itself to the flowers and, when you need to "refresh" the potpourri in the future, will reactivate when you simply add a few drops of the essential oil and toss again (it does not have to be stored again; it will be ready to use as soon as you add the additional essential oils).

You Will Need

3 cups dried botanicals (flower petals, pods, and leaves, mixed)
2 tablespoons orris root powder
12 drops essential oil

Tumble the botanicals to mix the blend. In a small pan (i.e. cake pan), spread out the botanicals in a layer that is about 1/4-inch deep. With a cheese shaker, shake a small amount of the orris root over the layer of botanicals. Then, put one drop of essential oil in four separate spots on the botanicals. Repeat until all of the botanicals are used up.

Dump everything into a large bowl. Put plastic gloves on and toss or mix. Put the whole mixture in a large container and let sit airtight and covered for about one and a half to two weeks. Then, take out and toss again.

Let the potpourri sit out in bowls to enjoy or pack in pretty bags and tie with a bow to give as gifts.

Foot Deodorizer Potpourri Sachet/Ball: Wintergreen and Peppermint

While this is great for freshening shoes overnight, you can also use one in kids' sock drawers—kids put dirty socks back in their drawers, trust me, I know this one…

You Will Need

1 cup rock salt
3 drops wintergreen essential oil
3 drops peppermint essential oil
1 drop spearmint essential oil

Using an eyedropper, add the essential oils to the salt and blend with spoon for about 30 seconds. Tie in fabric to make a sachet.

Shelf Life: 4 to 5 months; then refresh with essential oils again

Mother Nature Says …

Cut fabric swatches into either circles or squares, about 5 inches by 5 inches, to make balls by placing 1/2 cup of this formula in the center and gathering up the sides. Tie with a ribbon or bow to make a ball-shaped sachet.

POTPOURRI CLOSET FRESHENER: CITRUS AND SPICE, IT'S REALLY NICE...

This is natural and fun to make—a great project for kids to make and give at Christmas time. When my friend's kids did it as presents, the grandmas hung them on swags and on their trees as decorations until after Christmas when they moved them to their closets.

You Will Need

1 small orange
Full box of cloves
1 to 3 small cinnamon sticks
About 1 foot of ribbon

Poke cloves into the orange in a pattern of your choosing. Using a crossover method with ribbon (crossed at one end and then the other to secure the orange), make a hanging holder for the orange. At the top or second crossover (you may make as many crossovers as you like to make the hanger for your crossover secure), tie one or more cinnamon sticks on top. Use the rest of the ribbon to tie into a hanger on top.

Shelf Life: 1 to 3 months

All-in-one Linen and Sweater Protector and Cedar Chest Revitalizer

Do you know why sweaters and linens were so safe in an old cedar linen closet? It was the smell of cedar—moths just hate it! So, with the help of essential oil of cedarwood, you can make that old cedar chest or closet smell new again while protecting your sweaters and linens. You can either put it in fabric swatches like the Foot Deodorizer (see page 23), or tie it up in hankies to give as gifts. You can also use old nylon stockings: just cut a strip from one leg, stuff the rice in the center, and tie up both ends with ribbon or yarn.

You Will Need

1 cup white rice
6 drops cedarwood essential oil
1 drop orange essential oil

Add the essential oil to the rice and blend with spoon for about 30 seconds.

Shelf Life: Approx. 6 to 8 months (then can be refragranced again!)

Air Freshener

Want to make your own air freshener in a hurry? Add six to eight drops of essential oil to 4 ounces of water and put in a small spray bottle. Shake before using. This will store for about a month, so just make enough to use.

Are you a realtor or trying to sell a house? Do this with essential oil of cinnamon, and the home buyers will feel right at home with that "just-baked smell" in the house. Trying to neutralize a smell? Use vanilla essential oil. Trying to cover a smell? Use peppermint essential oil, or… the possibilities are endless!

Mother Nature Says …

OVER TIME, CEDAR CHESTS AND CLOSETS CAN LOSE THEIR WONDERFUL CEDAR SMELL, AND THE CEDAR WOOD WILL BECOME DRY. BY ADDING 10 DROPS OF CEDARWOOD ESSENTIAL OIL TO 1/4 CUP SWEET ALMOND OIL AND RUBBING IT HERE AND THERE INTO YOUR CEDAR CHEST, IT WILL REVITALIZE THE WOOD AND ADD THAT WONDERFUL CEDAR SMELL.

The Good Earth Bath, Beauty & Health Book

Chapter 3

Herbal and Botanical Remedies to Make You Feel Better

Herbs have been regarded as therapeutic since the beginning of recorded time. Used through the ages for food flavoring, natural treatments, purifying and ancient health cures, as well as treatments in a variety of beauty applications, herbs continue to be an important part of our world.

With traditional medicinal costs sky-rocketing and more and more questions being asked about drug safety and side effects, "alternative" medicine has gained more focus and visibility. Herbs are a very big part of today's natural alternative medicine. Research is accelerating on herb, plant, and botanical uses for common plants and herbs—and exotic ones that we are still discovering. If you look up any old-fashioned remedy or in a tribal medicine book, or talk to your grandparents, you will find herbs were used everywhere, by everyone, and for every purpose.

The following herbal home remedies were the result of research into both old and new plant and herbal experimentation and technologies, mixed with "old-time" remedies, some of which were furnished by the senior members of my own family.

I have stayed with the "providing comfort" side of the formulas and did not attempted to forge ahead into cures for major diseases. **For illness, you should see your doctor; further, you should consult your doctor before using an herbal home remedy, because reactions to certain foods or herbs can interfere with certain medications.**

What I want to share with you here are self-help formulas for everyday life that you can make at home, for the little inconveniences that you want to address yourself before they become major enough to warrant that expensive trip to the doctor. The advantages are that you can control both the costs and the materials used in the comfort of your own home, and you are in charge of your own well-being program; however, this is not a substitution for professional health care.

Picture this comfort from yester-year that we need more of today: Homemade cough drops and a pot of chicken soup, delivered to a homebound friend with the flu, are a loving and memorable gift for you both. It is a little of yesterday's warm loving touch—and just maybe something we need much more of today…

So, turn the following pages and enjoy the comforting thoughts of not only self-pampering, but of self-care and the natural healing and caring of those around you.

Good Health Tonic: Vinegar and Honey Drink

My grandfather swore by this one and made me drink it every day I stayed with him and my grandmother. This is a tonic for life, because it helps "balance" your body by providing both acid and alkali.

You Will Need

1 teaspoon honey
1 teaspoon apple cider vinegar
1 cup hot water

Dissolve the honey and vinegar in the hot water. Drink one glass daily.

BAD BREATH

Bad breath has two main causes: one is food odors left on the palate, such as onions or garlic, old food, or an acid/alkali imbalance in the mouth; the other is from your stomach (the sourness of your stomach actually affects your breath). The two mouthwash formulas are for food odors, and the other two are for odors caused by the stomach.

Peppermint Mouthwash

This is very similar to the mouthwash you pay big dollars for at the drugstore (without detergent in it, but who really wants to wash their mouth out with soap, anyway?). If you want it alcohol-free, just drop the peppermint extract in the water and leave out the alcohol.

You Will Need

1/4 cup 90-proof vodka or everclear
10 to 12 drops peppermint extract, food
   flavoring (food grade)
3/4 cup water (distilled)

Mix all together. Store in a dark glass bottle.

Shelf Life: With alcohol, 1 to 2 months. Without, use immediately.

Wintergreen or Cinnamon Mouthwash

Same as above, but substitute wintergreen or cinnamon extract, food flavoring (food grade) for the peppermint.

INTERNAL CLEANSING FOR BAD BREATH

There are some other great "side effects" of taking these internally besides helping with your breath: pepsin and comfrey will also help aid digestion, and liquid chlorophyll is a great blood builder.

Pepsin and Comfrey Pills

Found in health food stores, these really help clear the acids in your stomach, which sometimes can affect your breath. Take as prescribed. You could also put the pepsin and comfrey in the Lemon and Honey Drop formula (on page 35) for stomach soother drops.

Liquid Chlorophyll Diluted in Water

Take as prescribed (if you cannot find liquid chlorophyll, then look for pills).

BREATH MINTS

Use the formula and follow the directions for the Lemon and Honey Drops (see page 35) but substitute 1/2 teaspoon of peppermint extract (spearmint or wintergreen could be used as well) for the 1/2 teaspoon of lemon extract.

HOMEMADE TOOTHPASTE

Because we cannot preserve this at home, it is more of a "tooth powder" but is very effective. It is even a tooth whitener solution because both the abrasiveness of this formula and the flavoring extracts are strong enough to help whiten the teeth, as well as freshen the breath, as does the baking soda.

- 1/4 cup bicarbonate of soda (baking soda)
- 1 teaspoon table salt
- 1 tablespoon lemon peel (finely grated and dried)
- 1-2 drops of peppermint or wintergreen (or other) natural flavoring extract (food grade)

Mix together. Use a cheese or salt shaker to sprinkle on a wet toothbrush. Use as needed.

Shelf Life: 2 to 3 weeks

Natural Balm for Cold and Canker Sores

These are annoying problems that everyone hates. Although there are no cures for these recurring problems, this mixture will help them heal faster and you feel better. This is a great formula to make up and keep around the house during cold season, when it is needed most. This formula also is a great little healing balm that works on minor skin surface fungus infections.

You Will Need

1 tablespoon beeswax
1 teaspoon sweet oil
1/4 teaspoon camphor oil
1 acidophilus capsule (crushed)
1 800-unit Vitamin C capsule (crushed)

Melt the beeswax on low heat. Remove from heat; add the sweet oil, camphor oil, and crushed capsules and stir until the capsules' particles are dissolved and the mixture starts to cool and set up. Pour into little tins and let cool. Dab on cold sores or canker sores for relief.

Shelf Life: About 1 to 2 months

Bee Stings and Bug Bites

Bee stings and bug bites are irritating and itchy! This is caused either by a small amount of venom left in the skin or by the small skin injury of the "bite." Most bites and stings will settle down after a while (ice often helps the swelling), but the ingredients in the following formulas will help by soothing and calming the affected area, helping to give relief fast while the skin heals itself. If you are allergic to bee stings and show excessive swelling or puffiness in other parts of your body, call your doctor or seek medical attention right away.

Bee Sting Baking Powder Paste

This is good if you can get it on the bee sting ASAP. If you can get it on within a few minutes, it will pull a lot of burn and swelling from the site. If possible, put the "attacked" area in cold water while you are making this to hold the swelling down. Baking powder helps neutralize the toxins of the sting, and the chamomile will soothe the area as well, while the water is there to hold it together into a paste to keep it on the area. Leave on for 20 minutes, bathe again in cold water for 5 minutes, and then apply sweet oil to soothe and help heal.

You Will Need

1/4 cup baking powder
Water
3-4 drops chamomile essential oil or extract

Add just enough water to the baking powder to make a paste (usually about one-quarter to one-half the amount of the baking powder). Sift the essential oil into the powder. Add water a little at a time to make a paste.

Shelf Life: None; use and discard the rest

BUG BITE SOOTHER

It's the sweet oil and chamomile in this formula that provide the soothing, and the eucalyptus, thyme, and oregano provide the antiseptic and anti-inflammatory needs. Use on any bug bite to aid in healing and soothing relief. This has a great shelf life, so keep it on hand, especially in the summer.

You Will Need

1/4 cup sweet oil
5 drops eucalyptus essential oil
5 drops thyme essential oil
6 drops chamomile essential oil
5 drops oregano pure essential oil or
    extract

Mix all together and keep in a dark glass bottle.

Shelf Life: 5 to 6 months

HELP FOR RASHES

Whether it is heat rash or a slight allergy rash, this formula will help. If the rash continues or you run a temperature, see your doctor.

You Will Need

Gentle, unscented and uncolored lotion
1/2 teaspoon chamomile tincture (see
    page 18 for making tincture)
1/2 teaspoon evening primrose oil
4 drops stinging nettle tincture

Mix the tinctures and oil together. Mix with an equal part of the gentle, unscented and uncolored lotion. Spread on the skin. Wash off in 1 hour. Store in a cool place.

Shelf Life: 1 month

Mother Nature Says ...

YOU CAN FIND SWEET OIL AT MOST PHARMACIES. THE FIRST TIME I ASKED FOR IT, THE PHARMACIST ASKED WHAT IT WAS (HE HAD BEEN SELLING A LOT OF IT OVER THE COUNTER BUT WASN'T SURE WHAT IT WAS). SWEET OIL IS AN OLD NAME GOING BACK TO VICTORIAN TIMES WHEN IT WAS USED A LOT AS A MILD LUBRICANT AND BASE IN COSMETICS. IT IS THE FINEST QUALITY OF PURE OLIVE OIL AVAILABLE, SO IF YOU CAN'T FIND IT, GO TO A GOURMET SHOP AND BUY THE FINEST OLIVE OIL AVAILABLE. SWEET OIL IS A VERY CLEANED, REFINED OIL, AND SEEMS TO REALLY HELP THE SKIN HEAL, WHILE LETTING IT "BREATHE."

If you cannot find the tinctures or don't want to make one yourself, then try my grandmother's home formula. Both cabbage and onion seem to calm rashes. Besides my grandmother, I have seen other references to these as helps for rash; however, I cannot find out why, but it has always worked for me!

You Will Need

1 large cabbage leaf
1 large slice of onion

Mash the onion and rub the onion juices on the cabbage leaf. Apply the cabbage leaf to the irritated area.

Shelf Life: None; use and discard

FOOT ODOR DEODORIZER

This can be made into a spray or powder; I will give you a formula for both. The peppermint, wintergreen, and tea-tree work together as a mild anti-bacterial, as well as to combat foot odor.

You Will Need

4 drops wintergreen essential oil
4 drops peppermint oil essential oil
2 drops spearmint essential oil
4 drops tea-tree oil or extract

Spray

Add the essential oils and tea-tree oil or extract to 4 ounces of water. Put it in a spray bottle and shake before use.

Shelf Life: 1 month

Powder

Add the essential oils and tea-tree oil or extract to 1 cup of cornstarch or arrowroot powder by putting them on the cornstarch or arrowroot powder and forcing them through a hand-held flour sifter three or four times. Put in a cheese shaker and shake into tennis shoes.

Shelf Life: 6+ months

HEADACHE

The herbs listed in the next column combine analgesic, calming, alkalizing, anti-inflammatory, and decongestant properties useful for headaches. Make a homemade formula ready to use by combining equal amounts of these herbs to make a "headache" formula. The next time you have a headache try this:

Make an infusion (see page 14) or tea from this blend by steeping 1-1/2 tablespoons of the tea mix with 1-1/2 cups hot water (cover and steep for about 3 to 5 minutes). Pour 1/2 cup on a washcloth, then toss in the freezer to make cold (this will take 10 to 15 minutes). While you wait, lie down and sip the remaining tea (add some honey if you'd like).

Then lie down and put the washcloth on your head; rest for another 15 minutes or so. This formula will really help if it is a minor headache. If your headache should persist for more than one day, call your doctor.

Headache Tea Formula

Catnip
Chamomile
Comfrey
Lemon balm
Rosemary
Wintergreen

Mix equal amounts of the herbs and follow the directions above.

Mother Nature Says ...

OFTEN, SQUEEZING THE PEAK OF THE "V" IN THE SOFT SPOT BETWEEN YOUR THUMB AND FIRST FINGER WILL GIVE SOME RELIEF WHEN YOU HAVE A HEADACHE.

The Good Earth Bath, Beauty & Health Book

Sore Throat

Scratchy or sore throats result from an irritation of the mucus membranes in the throat. To soothe and help settle the irritation, the throat needs to be coated in a pleasant way. Here is a homemade sore throat and cough drop you can make and give as gifts during the cold season.

Here is my favorite herbal angle on this old-time, but effective, recipe. If you'd like, you can give this little recipe a lot more herbal, holistic punch by adding the following: 1 zinc tablet (crushed), 1 Vitamin C tablet, 1 Echinacea tablet, and 1 goldenseal tablet (if it is a capsule, just open and empty it into formula). Add these vitamins and herbs at the end, stirring them in just before you pour the formula into the pan to cool.

Lemon and Honey Drops

Remember that old phrase, "A spoonful of sugar makes the medicine go down?" Well, this works great with cough drops; plus, the sugar helps coat the throat along with the honey, which also soothes it. The lemon helps clear the phlegm and open the passageway. This is still a formula used in many commercial cough drops today.

You Will Need

1-3/4 cups sugar
1/4 cup honey
3/4 cup light corn syrup
1/2 teaspoon lemon extract
1/2 cup water

Line a 9 x 9-inch baking pan with aluminum foil (make sure the foil continues up the sides of the pan).

Butter the sides of a 2-quart saucepan. Combine the sugar, corn syrup, water, and honey in the pan. Cook and stir over medium-high heat until the mixture boils, stirring constantly to dissolve the sugar (about 4 to 6 minutes). Turn the heat down to medium and continue a light boil at a steady rate, stirring occasionally until a candy thermometer reads 290 degrees (soft crack stage). Continue to cook for 20 minutes, stirring occasionally.

Remove from heat and let cool; over the next 2 to 3 minutes, stir occasionally. Add the lemon (and other herbs and vitamins, if desired). Then, pour immediately into the foil-lined pan to cool. As it cools (another 3 to 10 minutes), you can use a spatula to "mark" your break lines into the cough drops (to make squares) in the approximate

sizes you want to have as single servings. The marks will stay when set up (if your marks do not stay, the mix is still too hot and needs to cool more; then try again).

Let set up overnight. Use the foil to lift out of the pan and break along the marks.

Package in individual candy wrappers. You can purchase these at cake decorating stores or candy crafting sections of a grocery store, but if you cannot find them, make your own out of wax paper. Store in a baggie or pretty paper sack until needed and in a cool, dark place.

Yield: 100 to 200 squares, depending on the sizes you mark and break.
Shelf Life: Up to 6 to 8 months, if properly wrapped and stored

EXPECTORANT COUGH SYRUP

Garlic and onions are tough on colds and fever, honey and glycerin help soothe the throat, vodka helps quiet the cough, and horehound has been used for almost 2,000 years for respiratory relief. If you have problems finding the leaves and flower tops of horehound, use horehound extract; if you do have the herb, see page 15 for making an extract. This formula will work without the horehound, but it's better with it. If this is for a child, you can leave out the vodka.

You Will Need

1 tablespoon chopped red onion
1/4 cup honey
1 tablespoon fresh lemon juice
1 tablespoon glycerin
2 tablespoons 90-proof vodka
1 teaspoon horehound extract (optional)

Warm the honey. Mix all together and shake well. Store in a cool place.

Shelf Life: With vodka, will keep for 2 weeks or more (can again be stored in the refrigerator). Without vodka, can be kept in the refrigerator for 3 to 4 days.

"COLDS" TEA

Wow—this ought to do it! This formula will help you make it through any cold a little easier. Echinacea and golden seal are lymph cleansing herbs, and rose hips are full of Vitamin C/BioFalvonoids. Pick up some capsules of Echinacea, golden seal, and rose hips at the health food store and take as directed. Then, make a tea using equal amounts of the following. If you cannot find all three of these teas, get teas of one or two and try adding a few drops of herbal extracts of the other(s) to the tea right before you make it.

Chamomile
Peppermint
Yarrow

Mother Nature Says ...

A SPOONFUL OF HONEY NOT ONLY MAKES THE MEDICINE GO DOWN, BUT ALSO THE COUGH! IF YOU HAVE A NIGHT COUGH, GET UP AND SWALLOW A SMALL AMOUNT OF PURE HONEY. A FEW DOSES WILL USUALLY SLOW YOUR COUGH.

NIGHT-TIME COLD FORMULA

Take an Echinacea and rose hips capsule before bed and then drink a little of this soothing night-time cold formula to help you sleep.

You Will Need

2 tablespoons lemon
1/4 cup corn syrup
1/4 cup hot water
2 tablespoons 90-proof vodka

Mix all together and drink slowly. Night-night!

KAVA KAVA FOR NERVES

Kava kava is a root that induces physical and mental relaxation and is helpful for anxiety- and stress-related disorders. There's no special formula here; just look in your health food store for capsules and follow the directions. **Caution:** This can cause drowsiness; do not operate cars or other machinery when using kava kava.

VEGETABLE JUICE LAXATIVE FOR CONSTIPATION

This formula is effective, good for you, and easy on the body.

You Will Need

1 cup tomato or V-8 juice
1/2 cup apple juice
1/4 cup sauerkraut juice
1/8 cup carrot juice

Mix all together and drink either before bed or the first thing in the morning.

TUMMY ACHE AND MILD UPSET STOMACH TEA

Peppermint contains menthol, which seems to soothe the muscle lining of the digestive tract. Drink this tea slowly to soothe your stomach. Peppermint tea is great for baby colic, too: dilute the tea to 1/4 peppermint tea with honey to 3/4 water. Make sure the bottle is not too hot (it should be just slightly warm). A little peppermint can help soothe a baby's tummy ache if it is given in a very mild dose. If the problem persists, call your pediatrician.

You Will Need

Peppermint herbal tea (caffeine free)
1 teaspoon honey

Make the tea as directed and add the honey.

Ginger Root and Papaya Elixir

Ginger root is known as a great stomach soother, and papaya is full of pepsin, a digestive aid. Together, they can provide relief to enzyme problems in the stomach.

You Will Need

1/4 cup honey
1 tablespoon alcohol
1 tablespoon water
1 ginger root capsule* (regular strength)
1 papaya capsule* (regular strength)

*It is important that the capsules are the gel types so that you can open and dump them into the honey and alcohol mix; otherwise, look for or make oils or infusions and add 1 teaspoon each.

Warm the honey until it is liquid. Mix all together.

Antiseptic Minor Wound Wash

This is so much less expensive than what you buy commercially and it is just as good. I like to make a larger amount and find a small bottle with a spray pump. You can take this with you when camping or anywhere where you might risk infection from a scrape in less-than-sanitary conditions. Wash the wound first, and then just spray or dab on. "Ouch" now, but you know what they say about an ounce of prevention (better than a pound of cure later…).

You Will Need

1/4 cup iodine
1 cup 90-proof vodka

Mix together and store in a dark glass bottle in a cool, dark place.

Shelf Life: 1 to 2 years

If you want to do away with iodine and alcohol, then mix this formula—it also works well!

You Will Need

1/4 cup tea-tree tincture (see page 18)
1 cup witch hazel

Mix together and store in a dark glass or plastic bottle in a cool, dark place.

Shelf Life: 8 months to 1 year

Help for Travel or Motion Sickness

Ginger tea or a piece of crystallized ginger will help calm the stomach and help prevent traveler's nausea.

HELP FOR BRUISES AND SPRAINS

Arnica tablets, available at health food stores, can be taken as directed to help bruises and sprains heal faster. Many surgeons now recommend this prior to surgery to help reduce bruising.

SUNBURN

Remember to monitor your time in the sun when using my Quick Tan oil (on page 71), or you will be mixing this for the after effects!

Quick Sunburn Calmer

You Will Need

Aloe vera gel
Plain yogurt
Apple cider vinegar

Mix equal amounts of the ingredients. Keep in a jar in the refrigerator. Shake before using. Use on burned areas once an hour for the first three hours.

Shelf Life: 1 to 2 weeks

ACNE

Acne is an inflammatory skin disorder that affects a lot of people. The sebaceous glands produce oil that lubricates the skin, and when these glands become over-active, they can produce acne. Dirt, dust, oils, and grime from pollution can add to the oil that the sebaceous glands are producing, so you can be assured of some problems. Tea-tree oil is a natural antibiotic and antiseptic, as is witch hazel, and wintergreen is an analgesic with the power to reduce inflammation. Here are my three favorites together in a dab-on solution.

Tea-tree Problem Spot Liquid

1 teaspoon tea-tree extract
2 teaspoons witch hazel
1/4 teaspoon wintergreen oil

Mix all together. Shake well before using. Dab directly on problem spots. Store in a bottle.

Shelf Life: 6 months

Mother Nature Says ...

WANT AN ANTISEPTIC TONER FOR YOUR WHOLE FACE? TAKE THE TEA-TREE PROBLEM SPOT LIQUID FORMULA AND ADD IT TO 1 CUP OF ADDITIONAL WITCH HAZEL AND 1 CUP OF WATER, AND YOU HAVE A GREAT FACE TONER. SHELF LIFE: 1 TO 2 MONTHS.

The Good Earth Bath, Beauty & Health Book

CHAPTER 4

The Scented Bath

In This Chapter:

Scented Gentle Bubble Bath

Luxurious Scented Bath Oil

Relaxing Bath Infusion

Body Butter

Herbal Bath Salts

Fizzy Bath Crystals or "Fizzy Shapes"

Old Fashioned Rose-water and Glycerin Bath

Oh, if I could sit by the sea all day, then soothe and luxuriate myself in a bath with exotic fragrances, and pass away the rest of the day in the waters of peace and tranquility…

For women, nothing has changed in the thoughts of bathing, relaxation, and pampering since Cleopatra's time. Today, however, women I run into say that they don't have time to bathe, so they always shower. They get a misty-eyed look when talking about what they think they don't have time for. Here's what I say: "When you're in the biggest push and don't think you have time for a hot bath is probably the time you need it most!"

So what turns bath time into a bathing ritual that becomes a sensory pleasure that is so important to your state of mind and health? Here is my prescription for turning your bath time into a relaxation ritual: Dim the lights and light some candles, roll a pillow from a towel or buy a bath pillow to support your neck as you lounge, play soothing music, use relaxing essential oils and a pampering bath product (see the formulas that follow), close your eyes, concentrate on your breathing, relax your muscles, listen to the music, smell the relaxing aroma, and luxuriate in the sensory of the warm water and silky products, improving your skin condition while you relax, relax, relax…

No worries—you are doing your part for your good health (by relaxing), the environment (you make these products yourself and they are safe and natural), and you did not have to take out a loan to enjoy the experience. Thank you, Mother Nature, for the water, aromas, and the relaxation…

Okay, okay, Cinderella, we've got some product formulas to cover before I lose you. There will be time for you to enjoy this after we make a few, so let's get started. First, review the aromatherapy examples on page 16 to help you decide which responses you want from your bathing experiences so you can add the ones you want wherever it says "essential oil of your choice."

SCENTED GENTLE BUBBLE BATH

You will get lots of big, gentle bubbles with this formula, and the glycerin will also help smooth your skin.

You Will Need

One 4-ounce gentle, unscented glycerin soap bar
1/2 cup water
1 teaspoon glycerin
1 teaspoon gentle baby shampoo (unscented if you can find it)
3-5 drops essential oil (your choice)

Melt the glycerin soap slowly in a double boiler on the stove. When melted, remove from heat and add the other ingredients. Stir for about 1 minute. Put in a pretty bottle and shake before using. Use about 1 to 2 teaspoons per bath.

Shelf Life: Approx. 2 to 3 months

Luxurious Scented Bath Oil

Scented oil is not only a delight but will also soothe and smooth your skin. If you have dry skin, you probably already love the delights of the skin softening and moisturizing that a fine bath oil can give you. But, the good ones are so expensive, so here is a superior formula that you can make at home without breaking the bank… This is also a great oil when you have over-dry skin from weather exposure.

You Will Need

1/2 cup apricot kernel oil
1 teaspoon jojoba oil
2 tablespoons olive oil
One 400-unit Vitamin E capsule (pierce it with a needle and squeeze the oil into the mix)
3-6 drops of essential oil (your choice)

Mix all together. Use 1 tablespoon per bath. Store in a bottle in a cool, dark place.

Shelf Life: 4 to 8 months

Relaxing Bath Infusion

Remember back on page 14 when we talked about infusions? Well, you could choose just about any herb, but here is a special relaxation formula I have designed for you. Lavender helps you relax and with dry, flaky skin. Peppermint will help revitalize you, the eucalyptus will help you breathe deeply, and the chamomile will help tone your skin and calm you. If you can't find the dried herbs, just add three drops of each essential oil to your bath for the same effect.

You Will Need

1 teaspoon peppermint
1 teaspoon lavender flowers (buds)
1 teaspoon eucalyptus leaves
1 teaspoon chamomile

Put all of the herbs in the center of a large square of cheesecloth. Gather and tie with a ribbon. Use hot water in your bath and let the herbs steep for about 5 minutes prior to getting in.

BATH BUTTER

Body and bath butters are becoming more popular. You can also use this formula for a deep tanning butter in the sun, but be careful: it will not only tan you quicker, it will also burn you quicker!

The temperature outside can affect this formula. If it is very cold, and the butter is too firm most of the time, simply re-melt and add more sweet almond oil until it stays soft when set up. If you're in a very hot climate and the butter stays melted all of the time, put it in the refrigerator to firm it up. The butter should be firm, yet you should still be able to spoon out a teaspoon full for your bath (it melts in the warm water).

You Will Need

1/2 cup cocoa butter
1/4 cup coconut oil
1 teaspoon sweet almond oil
3-6 drops essential oil (your choice)

Melt the cocoa butter in a double boiler on the stove. Add the coconut oil. When both are melted, remove from heat and add the sweet almond oil and essential oil. Stir until it starts to cool (5 minutes or so). Let set up (in the refrigerator, if you wish). Put in a decorative tin.

Shelf Life: 6 to 8 months

HERBAL BATH SALTS

Sea salt braces skin and helps "float" away impurities, while the baking soda soothes and smooths it and herbal oils add either herbal value or aromatherapy to the experience.

You Will Need

1/4 cup bicarbonate of soda (baking soda)

1/2 cup sea salt

3-4 drops of your favorite herbal essential oils

Mix the baking soda and sea salt together. Add the essential oils. Stir until mixed.

Shelf Life: 6 to 8 months

Fizzy Bath Crystals or "Fizzy Shapes"

You've seen them everywhere, usually pressed into little shapes. You can make this formula up and just toss it in your bath as is, or you can add a drop or two of sweet almond (or similar oil) to it, press it hard into a candy mold with your fingers (overfill the mold slightly), and then use a heavy book to finish compressing it into the mold overnight to set up the shape. Don't make too much at a time because it can react to moisture and get hard.

1/4 cup bicarbonate of soda (baking soda)
1/4 cup citric acid, powdered
3-4 drops essential oil

Mix the bicarbonate of soda and citric acid together. Add the essential oil. Store in a cool, dry place.

Shelf Life: 3 to 6 months

Mother Nature Says ...

If your mold falls apart, and looks dry and crumbly, use more oil. If it does not set up, and looks wet, you used too much oil. Using a fine mist sprayer, use one very light spray of water to help it set up, but this will give it a grainy appearance as water starts the fizzing action.

Old Fashioned Rose-water and Glycerin Bath

Together, rose water and glycerin were used in Victorian times as a skin softener and conditioner. Glycerin pulls moisture to the skin, and rose softens it. Here are all of the benefits of that skin softening preparation while you soak. Glycerin is water-soluble and does not leave a bathtub ring, so this is "clean" bath preparation as well. Also, this is a great gift idea: put it in a pretty, decorative bottle. Note: I like to add four or five drops of lavender essential oil to this to make it a rose-lavender bath. It is super relaxing!

You Will Need

1 cup glycerin
4-5 drops rose essential oil

Mix together. Shake before use. Store in a bottle.

Shelf Life: 4 to 8 months

The Good Earth Bath, Beauty & Health Book

Chapter 5

Massage Oils, Herbs, and Flowers in Oils and the Healing Touch ...

In This Chapter:

Super Moisturizing Massage Oil

Body and Anointing Oil

Beautiful Eucalyptus Rose Oil

Oil Exotique (Love Potion #9)

Tranquility Relaxing Oil

Stress is a common element in all of our lives these days. Dealing with stressful issues sets our ancient "fight or flight" reaction in motion, yet we're not able to release the pressure by doing either. When muscles become full of lactic acid buildup, and your mind is fatigued and unable to stand it any longer, it is time to unlock the stress with massage. Use the following products and information for a self-massage or share a massage with a friend.

Message Oils, Herbs, and Flowers in Oils and the Healing Touch ...

49

THE POWER OF CORRECT MASSAGE TECHNIQUES

Here are some professional tips to help you focus on feeling relaxed. To combine aromatherapy with body nourishing natural oils and human touch are very powerful relaxation tools, but breathing and water are also important elements to your massage program.

A holistic approach to reducing stress and improving your health and well being through massage is to use **deep breathing** to help you relax and focus your attention to the task at hand. Before starting, take a few slow, deep-cleansing breaths. While breathing, relax and focus on just your breathing while clearing your mind of any other thoughts.

Use natural oils for skin nourishing and creating "glide" on the skin to assist with massage. Using natural oils or crèmes helps promote the sense of well being, self-nurturing, and self-care. Cold pressed oils that maintain their natural vitamin content and nutritive values will not only lubricate your skin, but will also absorb into you when you are done, moisturizing your skin.

Aromatherapy assists by providing a "therapeutic" benefit, especially when combined with essential oils noted for evoking "relaxation" responses. It is just as helpful that the fragrance also brings to mind pleasant memories, which also stimulates positive and healing memory patterns (see page 16).

The power of caring human touch is a healing catalyst, both to help release tension and lactic acid buildup in the muscles. Touch is also a comforting, caring signal to the body and the mind. Use your hands, mind, and breathing together to focus on the muscles. Follow the directions in the next column for self-massage with the new oils and aromatherapy products you will create. When massaging, focus your attention and energy on the muscle groups as you work and exhale as you try to lengthen and stretch out tight muscles.

Water helps cleanse the body and remove toxins from it after the massage. Drink at least 8 ounces of water after your massage.

SELF-MASSAGE

First, start with 3 to 5 minutes of quiet time in a softly lit room. Start by focusing on the center of your diaphragm and quieting yourself by concentrating on your breathing. Keep your breathing slow and steady, breathing in through your nose and out through your mouth. Do not let yourself think of anything other than your breathing; push all other thoughts from your mind. When you are finally relaxed, it is time to start your self-massage.

Start with your feet. Using both hands and some massage oil, massage the bottom by applying pressure in a circular motion from the center of the foot. Then, massage upward on each foot, from the ankle to the toes, using your thumbs to press firmly. Massage each toe and then massage the tops of your feet, moving up your legs to the calves and upper legs. Apply oil as you work, using a kneading action on your sore muscles. Now, work on your neck and shoulders, starting on one side, using your fingertips. Work down your arms and then massage your hands and fingers.

Now that you are relaxed, brew up a scrub on page 82 or 83, working off dead skin cells, then rinse off and slip into a hot bath with bath salts on page 45. Emerge from your home massage and salon treatment a new person, ready again to take on the world.

SUPER MOISTURIZING MASSAGE OIL

This formula is for normal to very dry skin. It will make your skin feel amazing and give it lots of moisture.

You Will Need

1/2 cup sweet almond oil
1/4 cup coconut oil
4 tablespoons jojoba oil
1-1/2 tablespoons avocado oil
3-5 drops essential oil of your choice
    (either one or a combination)

Mix all together. Store in a cool, dry place.

Shelf Life: 3 to 6 months

BODY AND ANOINTING OIL

This formula can be used as a bath oil, an after-sun body oil, or as an anointing oil. It is moisturizing and nutritious for your skin, but not as "heavy" as the Super Moisturizing Massage Oil formula, so it will soak into your skin quicker. It is best for normal to oily skin.

You Will Need

1 cup apricot kernel oil
1/4 cup virgin olive oil
1 teaspoon wheatgerm oil
1 teaspoon jojoba oil
3-5 drops essential oil of your choice
    (either one or a combination)

Mix all together. Store in a cool, dry place.

Shelf Life: 4 to 8 months

Mother Nature Says ...

REMEMBER TO KEEP YOUR MASSAGE TIME QUIET. IF YOU NEED TO GO INTO THE BATH-ROOM TO RUN THE WATER FOR A BATH, LIGHT CANDLES AND PUT ON SOFT MUSIC. WITH A LITTLE PRACTICE, YOU WILL GET THE WHOLE PROCESS DONE IN 15 TO 20 MINUTES, THEN SLIDE INTO YOUR WARM BATH FOR ANOTHER 15 MINUTES AND SIMPLY SAVOR THE RELAXATION. IN A SHORT 30 MINUTES, YOU CAN EMERGE FROM THE BATH-ROOM, READY TO TAKE ON LIFE'S CHALLENGES.

BEAUTIFUL EUCALYPTUS ROSE OIL

Have you ever seen the beautiful bath and body oils with flower arrangements in them? Now you can do it yourself! In this formula, I have chosen eucalyptus and rose buds, but you can use other flowers; however, make sure they are safe for body contact by being completely dried and clean. Arrange the flowers in a beautiful see-through bottle and add the oils and essential oils. You can even decorate the bottle top, which makes it even more beautiful to look at—and to give as a gift. Use the Body and Anointing Oil formula on the previous page for this process because it gives the best movement of flowers and herbs in the bottle and has a good shelf life.

You Will Need

Body and Anointing Oil
1 small stalk eucalyptus (totally dried)
6-8 small rose buds (totally dried)
3-5 drops essential oil (rose or eucalyptus, or both)

Arrange the eucalyptus stem in a glass bottle in an attractive curve (the stem should be long enough to go from the bottom to the top so you can work with it but should stop just short of the cap). Toss in the small rose buds (at first they will raise to the top but in a few weeks some will get "saturated" and move to various levels in the bottle). Add a few drops of essential oil and the Body and Anointing Oil to the eucalyptus and rose buds. Shake two or three times, then cover with tight-fitting cap.

Shelf Life: 4 to 8 months

The Good Earth Bath, Beauty & Health Book

OIL EXOTIQUE (LOVE POTION #9)

The concept of this old formula has always been to attract men. Back in a day when pheromones didn't have a name, it was suspected an "animal" type scent would attract a man, and many combinations were put together in perfumes as "men attractors." The theory was to combine a little sweetness (rose) with a food scent that men find irresistible (vanilla), a strengthening smell for courage (vetiver) with musky, earthy smells to stimulate age-old carnal memories (patchouli and frankincense).

I love good frankincense; sometimes I dab a bit behind my ears before I go somewhere. My husband laughs because every time I do this, some man stops me and asks me what perfume I'm wearing (he wants to get some for his wife…). Play with different varieties of the oils listed below and you may just find your Love Potion #9!

Use the Body and Anointing Oil formula (on page 51) as a base.

You Will Need

Body and Anointing Oil
1 drop patchouli essential oil
1 drop vetiver essential oil
2 drops frankincense essential oil
2 drops rose essential oil
4 drops vanilla essential oil

Mix all of the essential oils together. Then mix with the Body and Anointing Oil. Store in a dark amber glass bottle.

Shelf Life: 4 to 8 months

TRANQUILITY RELAXING OIL

All of the following are for relaxation except for vanilla; it is a great blender because it helps "soften" the smells together. In fact, vanilla and jasmine are both great for this and therefore are used a lot to help "smooth" scents together to make it pleasing to the olfactory response. If you want to adjust the blend, keep this in mind. Use either the Super Moisturizing Massage Oil or Body and Anointing Oil formula (both on page 51) as a base.

You Will Need

Super Moisturizing Massage Oil or Body and Anointing Oil
3 drops lavender essential/fragrance oil
2 drops rose essential/fragrance oil
1 drop chamomile essential/fragrance oil
2 drops vanilla essential/fragrance oil
1 drop allspice essential/fragrance oil

Mix all together. Store in an amber glass bottle.

Shelf Life: 4 to 8 months

The Good Earth Bath, Beauty & Health Book

CHAPTER 6

Soapcrafting: Feeling Creative?

In This Chapter:

Basic Soap Molding

Oatmeal and Lavender Soap

Toy or Decal in Soap

Soap by the Slice

Soap crafting is an ancient art that is about as old as candlemaking. It remained the same for many years with the only variations being colors, smells, and additive ingredients like abrasives for scrubbing, moisturizers, and so forth

Today, we have taken a time-honored craft and had some fun looking at it as an art medium. I like to call this "functional art" because you can be artistic with something that you will use, in the same spirit that fine food gourmets do with food presentations. Functional art… I think Mother Nature would approve, because she has always used that concept…

Have you ever seen or bought "soap by the slice?" Or what about those cute clear soaps that have toys or decals inside that sparkle through the clear soap, beckoning like the toy

prize in a Cracker Jack box? Want to make some seashell or angel soaps to give as gifts or decorate your bathroom?

I am not going to teach you how to make soap here because it is a rather tedious process using lye that can be dangerous to do at home (and there are already many good books about soap making on the market, including *The Complete Soapmaker*, by Norma Coney, *Transparent Soapmaking*, by Catherine Failor, and *Soap*, by Ann Bramson). Instead, I'm going to share techniques with you so that you can buy soap and make all of those fun little "tricks" you've seen. If you have kids, these are great do-at-home crafting projects. So, gather everyone around and get ready to do four simple, fun projects with soap.

These projects are all done with clear natural glycerin soaps that can be found anywhere. Remember to buy quality glycerin soap; those that are not of high quality will not mold well. A quality glycerin is a moisturizing soap that lends itself well to the "melt and pour" concepts that I will show you here, and you can still say you made it yourself (kind of like making chocolate shapes on a stick). Once you start this creative process, it can be addicting!

You have a choice here if you want to color or fragrance the soap on your own; if you do, buy some that is unfragranced and uncolored. Otherwise, if you buy soap that is already colored and scented (like in the case of molding only and you like that color and fragrance), it's okay to leave it as is. You may find that you lose a little of the fragrance in the melting process, so you can add a little more.

You Will Need

Double boiler (glass is best so you can see
    what's going on, but others will work)
Stainless steel spoon
Quality natural clear glycerin soaps
Food colorings
Essential oils of your choice
For soap by the slice:
Plastic bread keeper or loaf pan
Plastic square or rectangular container
Knife
Electrical gloves (electricians use these to
    protect their hands)
Thin- to medium-gauge metal wire (cut
    no more than about 12-15 inches)
For molded soaps:
Plastic or rubber candy molds
For toys or decals in soaps:
Small plastic or rubber toys
Coated decals
Plastic ice cube trays or single-serving
    milk cartons

Basic Instructions and Troubleshooting: Read This First!

Here is some information about what can go wrong with melt and pour techniques:

1. When you are fragrancing (with essential oils, of course), try not to add more than 1 percent of the essential oil to the soap. In simple terms, do not add more than about 3 or 4 drops per 4-ounce soap bar that you are melting. If you over-fragrance, you can upset the balance of the soap and it will not reset properly. Remember, a little goes a long way with essential oils. When choosing a fragrance to use, make sure it is a good quality essential oil; do not use perfume or cologne because it is too diluted and will not give you enough fragrance for the amount you use, and to use more would just overload the soap.

2. Do not bring the soap to a boil in **any form**; keep the burner on low even if it takes a little time to melt. Even a few bubbles can ruin the soap (it gathers too much moisture when it sets up). People sometimes ask me if they can use the microwave for this process. The answer is yes, **but** remember what I said about the boiling issue. Be prepared to ruin a couple of batches until you get your microwave's temperatures figured out—the boiling point happens so fast in a microwave!

3. Do not be tempted to put your newly poured soap in the refrigerator to set up; this also gathers moisture and later your soap will look like it's crying. Just let the soap set up in a cool, dry place overnight. If it's very humid, let it set up in an air conditioned room, away from the air conditioner; otherwise, room temperature is fine.

4. Do not add essential oil when the soap is at its hottest. Let the melted mixture sit for 3 to 5 minutes while you stir, then add the essential fragrance and color. Essential oils are like vitamins: they lose some of their effectiveness in high heat. Many a professional soapmaker has called me with problems of their fragrance not "holding." Most of the time, the problem is that they have simply "cooked" the fragrance right out of their batch when they are making the soap. Technique is everything in this industry!

5. You can use grocery store food coloring to color your soaps, but be advised that even though they are safe to use they are water soluble and will wash off if you get them on you (this may take a day or two if it gets on your skin at full strength). The bottom line? Keep your soap colors pastel. The question I get asked so frequently is: "How much color do I use?" While it seems like a logical question, and indeed I can give exact answers for everything else, my answer probably leaves the person feeling a little silly: What shade do you want it, what is the volume size, and how dark do you want it? Color is subjective. In other words, you have to just play with this. Yes, you can mix colors together like paint colors (red and blue make purple, yellow and red make orange, blue and yellow make green, and so on), but be creative! My main warning on color is go easy on the amount you add and stay with pastels. Even though this color is safe, no one wants to use a midnight blue soap and then try to wash a second time to get the color off his or her hands. Again, a little goes a long way with colors; for a 4-ounce bar, one drop of food coloring will give you a pretty, medium shade.

6. Use only plastic and rubber molds. For molded soaps, you can use those cute plastic candy molds you find at craft and cake decorating stores. Plastic "flexes" and allows you to unmold easily when the soap is set up. Do not use metal and especially don't use plaster molds because the soap soaks right into it and tries to moisturize the poor dry plaster! Milk cartons that have been waxed and can be "torn away" are okay, too. You will know your soap is set up because it is dry enough to pop out with just a little encouragement (twisting). The bigger the soap mold, the longer the set-up time. When you unmold your creation, air dry for just a few hours, then wrap in plastic until ready to use (glycerin loves to pull moisture from the air to your skin; if there is no skin, it will accumulate moisture all by itself). If it is to be a gift, put it in a plastic bag, tie the top with a ribbon, and store in a cool, dry place (soaps have a very long life).

Okay, now that you understand the basic dos and don'ts, its time to play!

Mother Nature Says ...

If you ever have a really stubborn soap mold that won't release, dip it in hot water, like you may do with Jell-O. The heat will ever-so-slightly melt what's sticking, and you should then be able to twist the mold to get it to release. Glycerin is naturally a little more slippery, so this is usually not an issue unless you have dried out the soap with too high of heat or too many meltings. Soap loses a little moisture every time it's melted.

BASIC SOAP MOLDING

This is the simple melt-and-pour method.

You Will Need

Soap*
Color and essential oil, if desired

*You can use either clear glycerin soap or opaque (white soap) for this method.

Melt the soap base slowly on low heat. Once it is melted, remove from heat (this is where you add the color and fragrance after a short cool-down, if you wish). Next, simply pour the soap into the candy molds. Let sit overnight or until the mold pops out easily. Wrap in plastic, or take straight to your bathroom for use. Wasn't that easy?

OATMEAL AND LAVENDER SOAP

Experiment and have fun with this beautiful soap. The oatmeal can give you a layered look, but it can be accomplished with almond, orange, or lemon pieces and herbs. There are two methods for creating this soap. For either method, you can use a pan (and cut slices of soap per the instructions on page 61) or you can use a mold.

You Will Need

Soap*
Lavender flowers
Oatmeal, grated

*You can use either clear glycerin soap or opaque (white soap) for this method.

Method 1 (not shown): Melt the soap base slowly on low heat. Add lavender flowers and stir into the soap. Pour the soap into a pan. When the soap is starting to set up, stir in grated oatmeal; usually, the oatmeal will "float" throughout the soap, which will give you a layered look.
Method 2 (shown below): Melt the soap base slowly on low heat. Put the lavender flowers and oatmeal in the bottom of the pan. Pour the soap over the lavender flowers and oatmeal.

TOY OR DECAL IN SOAP

This works better with no color added, but if you want color, use a very, very pastel or you won't see the toy or decal inside well. A lovely Cameo decal in soap makes a charming gift for grandma. Do you know someone who collects animals? Give him or her a darling animal soap—like the frog shown here—for the bathroom. A mom will thank you when you give soap with a toy in it—what will her child have to do to get the toy? *Wash*, of course. Maybe we can trick little Johnny into that bath after all…

Want rainbow or two-color soap? Follow the same layering process described here but don't put anything in it, just color each layer a different color. You can even use essential oils to make each layer a different, but synergistic, therapy smell… Are you feeling creative yet?

You Will Need

Clear glycerin soap
Essential oil, if desired
Rubber or plastic toys your choice (these must fit into the soap mold and be no more than half the size of the mold)
Or
Coated, two-sided decal

Melt the soap base slowly on low heat. Remove when melted. If desired, add fragrance.

You do not want to just set the item in the bottom of the mold, because when you unmold, it won't really be "suspended" in the soap (it will be just sadly sitting on the bottom). To suspend items in soap, you must first create a soap "stand" for the item within the soap. This means that you will be pouring some of your soap base now, and re-melting the rest and pouring the balance of your melted soap later.

If you are putting in a toy, decide by the size of the toy where you will want it height-wise in the soap. Pour the first layer of soap just a little under that height.

If you are putting in a decal, pour the soap to fill half of the mold.

Let the first layer of soap set up until it is mostly firm and will easily hold the item you want to place in the middle. If you leave it until it is totally set up and dry on top, the two layers of soap will not stick together, yet at the same time, you want it to be firm enough to hold and not "break through" when you pour the next layer. The best time is when it is almost completely set up, all firm, with just a slight bit of moisture on top. (I wish I could give you an exact time, but it depends on the size of the mold.)

Now remelt the base again on low heat, set the toy or decal in place, and slowly spoon the melted soap over the item until enough depth is achieved that you can gently pour the rest up to the top. With any luck, you will only have to do two stages, not three, unless that's what you desire.

Mother Nature Says ...

USUALLY, THE TOY STAYS WHERE IT IS, BUT OCCASIONALLY, YOU GET A "FLOATER," ESPECIALLY IF THE TOY IS HOLLOW AND FILLED WITH AIR. NOT TO WORRY; JUST USE A MEAT BASTER TO REMOVE SOME OF THE SECOND SOAP POURED. LET'S SAY YOU'RE USING A BOY FIGURE. LEAVE HIS FEET COVERED WITH THE SECOND POUR, JUST ENOUGH TO COVER THEM, BUT NOT ENOUGH THAT HE IS FLOATING. LET THAT SET UP. THEN, WITH HIS FEET STUCK IN THE LAST SOAP LAYER, YOU CAN REPEAT THE PROCESS AND HE WON'T FLOAT. THE SAME PROCESS WORKS FOR FLOATING DECALS: JUST LET THEM FLOAT IN A VERY SMALL AMOUNT OF SOAP IN THE MIDDLE AND THEY WILL SET UP. NOW POUR THE TOP LAYER.

SOAP BY THE SLICE

We've all seen them and, boy, are they expensive! How are all of those textures and shapes and the different looking soaps made? Here's how—and you don't even need to be a pro to do this at home. Again it is simply technique when you use both clear glycerin soap and opaque (white) soap.

For this first one, we will be suspending opaque soap chunks in clear soap, but once you get the hang of this, you will want to try it many different ways to see the patterns, like those shown in the samples, you can create.

You Will Need

1 to 2 lbs. clear glycerin soap
8-12 ounces opaque (white or non-clear) soap
Color
Essential oils

First, divide the opaque soap into three equal portions. Melt each portion separately. Take the first opaque portion, melt it on low heat on the stove, color it (your choice), and pour it into a plastic square or rectangular container.

After it sets up, unmold and use the knife to cut into uneven "chunks." Repeat this process with the other two portions of opaque soap, coloring each a different color. Set them aside until needed.

Take the full amount of clear glycerin and melt it on low heat. Meanwhile, arrange a few (one half to one third) assorted colors of chunks at random in the bottom of a plastic loaf pan. When the clear glycerin is melted, you have a decision to make. You will be pouring this into the pan around the opaque chunks. If you pour it while it is very hot, it will make more of a chunk and marbled effect because some of the chunks will melt (if not all). If you want to see the chunks clearly, let the clear base cool for 15 to 20 minutes before pouring or spooning in. Pour just enough to cover the tops of the chunks. Now, if you like this height you can stop here, but usually it is too short. Either way, you must wait for this layer to set up until firm, but still slightly moist on top (if you are going to layer again; otherwise, see the next part).

Repeat the whole process one or two more times until you are getting the "height" you want for your soap loaf.

When totally set up (this is a lot of soap and set up can take 1 to 3 days, depending on depth), take the soap out of the loaf pan.

Now it's time to cut the slices (this is not for children). With the knife, just score (do not cut the slices now) lines for how thick you want the slices by making a small mark along the side of the bar (like cutting a bread loaf). With glycerin soap, if you try to cut it with a knife, it will splinter (this was okay with chunks because we did not care if they were perfect). We want beautiful perfect slices, so turn a stove burner on medium high and put on your heavy electrical gloves. Take a thin- to medium-gauge metal wire, enough to stretch across the burner you will use and leave your hands

free of the burner, and still have enough to wrap the wire around your gloved hand one time at each end for a sure grip. Hold the wire briefly on the burner after it is on full heat (mind your gloved hands). It will take only about 5 to 10 seconds for the wire to get very hot because metal conducts heat very well (and the reason you need to protect your hands with adequate coverage at both ends of that wire). Using the marks where you have scored the soap, quickly slice the soap using the whole width of the hot wire. It will cut beautifully and you will get to see the treasures inside that were made during the pouring process.

Now that you understand this concept, you do not have to stay with "chunks"; you can use molds to mold shapes and then suspend them. Try putting strips of one colored opaque in another color of opaque base, or do the same with transparent. Play with different looks and shapes and have fun!

How does it look if you shred some of the soap? You can use all of the techniques I have taught you in the other two processes in making unique, soap by the slice…

The Good Earth Bath, Beauty & Health Book

Herbal/Botanical Shampoos and Conditioners: Bubble, Bubble, Toil, and Trouble (well, not too much trouble...)

In This Chapter:

Gentle Herbal/Botanical Shampoo
For Normal Hair
For Dry and Damaged Hair
For Oily Hair

Hair Dry Cleaner

Anti-dandruff Rinse

Tea-tree Anti-dandruff Rinse

Herbal/Botanical Hot Oil Treatment

Herbal/Botanical Protein Dry Hair Deep Conditioning Pack

The nice thing about natural ingredients is that they are usually both gentle and safe for all hair types, including color-treated hair. Avoid shampoos that have detergent as the base; instead, look for gentler formulas with lots of natural ingredients. Here are a few natural "kitchen formulas" that you can whip up yourself!

GENTLE HERBAL/BOTANICAL SHAMPOO

This is a gentle formula that everyone can use. The thing that makes it suitable for dry, normal, or oily hair is the herbal/botanical essential oils or ingredients you add to it. When the formula calls for a "shampoo base," you can use one of two variations: Liquid Castile Soap (a very mild, olive-oil based soap) that is low sudsing, or unscented and uncolored baby shampoo that is more sudsing. Both are mild and will make a great "starter" for your homemade product. For all formulas, use about the size of a quarter in the palm of your hand. Combine with water to lather and apply to hair. Lather, rinse, and repeat, if necessary.

Mother Nature Says ...

IF YOU CANNOT FIND LIQUID CASTILE SOAP, BUY WHITE, PURE, SOLID CASTILE SOAP AND USE A GRATER TO SHRED. THEN, MIX WITH AN EQUAL AMOUNT OF WATER (SHAKE SEVERAL TIMES TO MIX), BUT BEFORE YOU SHAKE, BE SURE THAT THE BOTTLE IS CORKED AND ONLY HALF FULL (THERE WILL BE LOTS OF BUBBLES!). KEEP SHAKING UNTIL THE SOAP DISSOLVES.

FOR NORMAL HAIR

This blend will gently cleanse but not strip hair: the herbs used here will clarify the hair and scalp and help add shine. The glycerin and white vinegar will help it rinse clean so that there is no residue left in your clean, shiny hair. This is the equivalent to a natural herbal shampoo that you might buy, but better and more cost effective, because you made it yourself.

You Will Need

1 cup "shampoo base"
1 teaspoon glycerin
3 drops rosemary essential oil
3 drops sage essential oil
1 teaspoon white vinegar

Mix all together. Store in a pretty bottle.

Shelf Life: Approx. 3 to 6 months

FOR DRY AND DAMAGED HAIR

This formula has lots of enriching oils and herbs that are soothing and conditioning. This will help impart that silky feeling back into your hair.

You Will Need

1 cup "shampoo base"
1 teaspoon glycerin
1 teaspoon aloe vera
1 teaspoon jojoba oil (or apricot kernel oil)
3 drops chamomile essential oil
3 drops lavender essential oil
1 Vitamin E capsule, 400 units or more (pierce and put in formula)

Mix all together. Store in a pretty bottle.

Shelf Life: Approx. 3 to 6 months

FOR OILY HAIR

Here we want to "brace" the scalp and slow down oil production a little, without being too harsh. If you totally strip the scalp, it will only signal it to produce more oil, and we want to remove all excess oil without over-drying.

You Will Need

1 cup "shampoo base"
1 teaspoon glycerin
1/2 teaspoon tea-tree extract or oil
1/2 teaspoon nettle extract or oil (fir nettle is okay, too)
1/2 teaspoon witch hazel
3 drops each of two kinds of essential oils: orange, frankincense, grapefruit, lemon, juniper, cypress, borage, or lavender

Mix all together. Store in a pretty bottle.

Shelf Life: Approx. 3 to 6 months

HAIR DRY CLEANER

A 50/50 blend of cornstarch and baking soda makes a quick dry shampoo for oily hair. Using a handheld flour sieve, sift the two together until blended. If you want, add a few drops of essential oil during the sifting process for a just-shampooed smell (rosemary, pine, and juniper give hair a wonderful fresh, clean smell, and each also removes oil from hair). This makes a great dry shampoo for oily hair when you don't have enough time to shower.

Put in a shaker, shake a small amount on your hair, then brush until the powder is gone. When you brush out the powder, it takes the hair's oil with it!

Shelf Life: 2 years

DANDRUFF

Dandruff is a common scalp condition that occurs when dead skin is shed, producing white skin flakes most often called seborrhea (which is an inflammatory skin disease caused by a problem with the sebaceous, oil secreting glands). Increase your B-complex vitamins and try this anti-dandruff after-shampoo rinse.

Anti-dandruff Rinse

The vinegar works as a mild astringent, which needs to be diluted (especially for those of you with colored hair). Thyme also helps tone the scalp.

You Will Need

1/4 cup apple cider vinegar
4 cups water
1 cup thyme infusion (make thyme tea with 1 teaspoon thyme steeped in hot water, covered for 5 minutes)

Mix all together and use (about half, depending on the length of your hair) as a rinse after shampooing. Store in a dark glass bottle in a cool, dark place.

Shelf Life: About 1 week

Tea-tree Anti-dandruff Rinse

Tea-tree and witch hazel are both astringents that help clear the skin of flakes and discourage the scalp from forming more dandruff.

You Will Need

1/4 teaspoon tea-tree extract
1/4 cup witch hazel
4 cups water

Mix together and use (about half, depending on the length of your hair) as a rinse after shampooing. Store in a bottle.

Shelf Life: About 2 weeks

HERBAL/BOTANICAL HOT OIL TREATMENT

This is a salon-quality hot oil treatment. It is fabulous on very dry hair; if you have oily hair, don't use it.

You Will Need

1/4 cup virgin olive oil
1 Vitamin E capsule, 400 or more units (pierce and squeeze contents into mix)
1 tablespoon coconut oil
1 tablespoon jojoba oil
3 drops lavender essential oil
1 drop rosemary or cedarwood essential oil

Mix all together. Put on towel-dried hair after shampooing. Leave in for 5 to 10 minutes and then wash out. Store in a bottle.

Shelf Life: 2 to 3 months

HERBAL/BOTANICAL PROTEIN DRY HAIR DEEP CONDITIONING PACK

This is like a mudpack for your hair without the mud. It's full of deep conditioners that are great for all hair types if used once a month.

1 tablespoon coconut oil
1/8 cup sweet almond oil
1/8 cup aloe vera gel
3 tablespoons gelatin mix*
2 drops geranium essential oil
3 drops bay or rosemary essential oil

*Mix 1 tablespoon of unflavored gelatin in 2-1/2 tablespoons of cold water. Stir. Put in microwave to heat water to boiling and then stir again.

Mix all together and stir. Put on towel-dried hair after shampooing. Leave in for 5 to 10 minutes and then wash out.

Shelf Life: None; use immediately

The Good Earth Bath, Beauty & Health Book

Chapter 8

Lotions and Potions: Formulas to Soften You Up ...

In This Chapter:

Light, Creamy Lotion for
Normal to Oily Skin

Body Butter Crème
for Dry Skin (or Dry Climates)

Minty Cleansing Cold Crème

Vitamin E Under-eye Treatment

Quick Tan Oil

Lotions and potions, potions and lotions, just fun to say isn't it? But for us, it's serious business. We are the fairer, softer sex, and we really have to work hard to maintain that title! There are so many choices at the counter that it can be difficult to choose. Well, now you can make a few moisturizers and creamy soft cleansers yourself... This chapter will show you how to stay soft and supple on the outside in today's "tough as nails" environment.

This chapter is dedicated to my friends in the desert. Mother Nature's beauty is rare there indeed—the desert has its own special beauty, but that dry climate means dry skin. We all need moisturizers, but our friends in the desert buy twice as much moisture lotions as anyone else, so check out the Body Butter formula—this one's for you!

LIGHT, CREAMY LOTION FOR NORMAL TO OILY SKIN

This is a great body lotion. The combination of beeswax and oils with aloe will moisturize without being too heavy on the skin.

You Will Need

1/4 cup aloe vera gel
1/8 cup beeswax
1/2 cup apricot kernel oil
4 drops of essential oils (your choice)
4 drops jojoba oil
3 teaspoons borax

Melt the apricot kernel oil, jojoba oil, and beeswax together in a small pan. In a separate bowl, mix the aloe vera gel and borax together until the borax is dissolved. When the beeswax is melted into the oils, remove from heat. Stir a couple of times and then slowly stir in the aloe-borax mixture. Keep stirring for about 5 minutes, then add the essential oils. Continue stirring for about another 2 minutes. Put in cute little tubs or bottles.

Shelf Life: Keep in the refrigerator; it will be good for a few weeks

Mother Nature Says ...

IF THE MIXTURE IS TOO THIN, REHEAT IT A LITTLE, ADD MORE MELTED BEESWAX, AND STIR. IF THE MIXTURE IS TOO FIRM, REHEAT IT, ADD MORE APRICOT KERNEL OIL, AND STIR.

BODY BUTTER CRÈME FOR DRY SKIN (OR DRY CLIMATES)

Today, body butters are very popular. Cocoa butter is the original body butter and is a terrific moisturizer all by itself (I never go to Hawaii without it; great after-tan stuff). Here is a formula that uses cocoa butter, shea butter (if you can find it), and natural oils to make a special butter for you. This is the one for my desert friends.

You Will Need

1/4 cup aloe vera gel
1/4 cup cocoa butter (or, if you can find shea butter, use 1/8 cup shea and 1/8 cup cocoa butter)
1 tablespoon olive oil
4-5 drops essential oil of your choice

Melt the oils together on low heat. Remove from heat and stir in the aloe vera gel and essential oils. Stir for about 1 to 2 minutes. Put in cute pots or tins with lids.

Shelf Life: 3 to 6 months

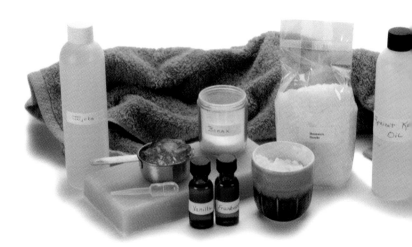

MINTY CLEANSING COLD CRÈME

This will work as a grime and make-up remover. The oil and vegetable shortening will glide off dirt and make-up, the aloe will soothe and help cut the oils, and the mint will also help take the oils off and tone the skin.

You Will Need

- 1/4 cup vegetable shortening (the thick vegetable-derived kind, not animal)
- 1/4 cup aloe vera gel
- 1 teaspoon olive oil or avocado oil
- 1-2 drops essential oil of peppermint or spearmint, or both

Warm the vegetable shortening until it melts. Remove from heat. Let cool for 2 to 3 minutes and then fold into the aloe vera gel. Add the olive or avocado oil and keep folding for 1 minute. Add the essential oils and stir for another minute. Put in cute tins or jars and store in the refrigerator.

Shelf Life: Approx. 2 weeks

VITAMIN E UNDER-EYE TREATMENT

It takes a powerful moisturizer to combat deep facial lines. Vitamin E (alpha tocopherol) molecules penetrate the epidermis to reach the base skin tissues. It has long been used for firming, tightening, and moisturizing and can postpone and lessen wrinkles. You cannot use other oils that are heavier because it will soak in and "build-up" under your eyes and sometimes cause puffiness. Vitamin E is a light oil, but strong enough to moisturize the fine lines around eyes and mouth, as well as under-eye wrinkles. This is also great for fine lines other places on your face. Do not be tempted to mix essential oils with this; they are too strong for around eyes and mucus membranes.

Snip a capsule of d-alpha tocopherol (make sure it is natural Vitamin E, not synthetic). Add equal amounts of straight Vitamin E from the capsule with aloe vera oil (equal to or more than the amount of Vitamin E) and dab it under your eyes at night before bed and let dry.

You can make up 1 to 2 ounces and store in a dark glass bottle or tin in a cool, dry place.

Shelf Life: 2 weeks

QUICK TAN OIL

This oil comes with a warning: It will tan you quicker, but it will also burn you quicker! This formula in not for "virgin skin" because it contains no sunscreens; it is for an already tanned person who wants to make 15 to 20 minutes in the sun have the results of 30 to 40 minutes. It is also a great "after sun" moisture oil that keeps the skin from looking dry and peeling. If you wish, you can also add a few drops of your favorite essential oil.

You Will Need

- 1/2 cup sweet almond oil
- 1/4 cup jojoba oil
- 2 tablespoons wheat germ oil

Mix all together. Store in a bottle in a cool, dry place.

Shelf Life: Approx. 6 months

The Good Earth Bath, Beauty & Health Book

Chapter 9

Facial Treatments, Masks, and Steams: It's Spa Time!

In This Chapter:

Anti-oxidant Facial Treatment

Soy Mask With Mint

The Good Earth Facial Mask from Cucumber and Green Clay

Rosemary's Creamy Milk Facial

Spa-type Aromatherapy Facial Steam

Make-up Remover for Face and Eyes

Eyelash Conditioner

Eye Balm (Wrinkle Reducer)

Treat yourself to a home spa treatment—you deserve it. Long before the "spa concept" was even developed, women would gather together to brush each other's hair and share beauty secrets. Have a sleepover with some of your friends. You're never too old to sleep over with the girls, do each others' hair, tell stories and giggle, and while you're at it, whip up a couple of these great treatments. You may look silly sitting around the kitchen table, but you'll feel fabulous in the morning (providing you don't tell those stories too late into the night…). If we did a little more of this, I think physicians would dispense a little less valium! Mother Nature gave us all of the tools to be beautiful and time to relax, but it's up to us to use them…

ANTI-OXIDANT FACIAL TREATMENT

Vitamin C is an anti-oxidant that helps clear the skin of "free radicals." This creates a very slight "peel" effect. The result is glowing, fresh skin that is clear of free radicals, ready to moisturize, and face the world.

You Will Need

3 teaspoons pectin
1/8 cup hot water
1/4 teaspoon lemon juice
1/8 teaspoon Vitamin C crystals (or powder)
1/8 teaspoon liquid glycerin

Dissolve the pectin in the hot water. Add the rest of the ingredients to the water. Stir. Use your fingers to pat on your face. Cover with a muslin or gauze sheet and wait for 10 minutes. Rinse off with water.

Shelf Life: None; make and use

SOY MASK WITH MINT

This is a good mask for all skin types, but it is particularly good for dry skin because it does not over-dry it. The peppermint essential oil will clarify the skin.

You Will Need

1/4 cup soy powder
1/4 cup unflavored yogurt
1 to 2 drops peppermint essential oil

Mix the soy powder and unflavored yogurt to make a paste, then add the peppermint essential oil. Pat on your face and let sit for 30 minutes. Rinse off with water. Look at the glow…

Shelf Life: None; make and use

The Good Earth Facial Mask from Cucumber and Green Clay

Some earth clays do great things for your skin. My favorite is green French Clay, available at most health food stores. Cucumber has a coloring effect and will soothe the redness that sometimes develops when using a pore-tightening mask. The water is just to make the clay moist and spreadable, while the sweet almond oil adds some moisturizing effects to the mix. This is great for reducing pores.

Mother Nature Says ...

When making this mask, if it is too chunky for application, simply add more water; if it is too runny, add more clay. If you want it to be more of a facial conditioning pack, add more oil (this is great for dry skin), but go easy on the oil if you have oily skin.

You Will Need

1/8 cup French Clay
1 medium cucumber, peeled and mashed
Water (enough to make into a paste)
1 teaspoon sweet almond oil

Mix the French Clay, cucumber, and oil together in a bowl. Use the water to make a very moist paste (a medium cucumber will vary in moisture level so you will just have to add enough water to make a very soft clay). Put on your face and let sit until dry, usually 10 to 15 minutes (the moisture will evaporate from the mask, causing a "pulling" action, which presses out whiteheads/blackheads from your skin and tightens your pores). Wash off and enjoy your beautiful tight, glowing skin.

Shelf Life:
None; make and use

ROSEMARY'S CREAMY MILK FACIAL

This is an amazing moisturizing facial right from your kitchen.

You Will Need

1/4 cup mayonnaise
1/8 cup honey
4 tablespoons powdered milk
2 drops rosemary essential oil

Heat the honey to make it easy to mix, then blend it with the mayonnaise, powdered milk (do not add water to the milk, use it in its powdered state), and rosemary oil. If it is warm from the honey, let it cool a few minutes first, then stir again and apply to your face. Let sit for 15 minutes, then wash off.

Shelf Life: None; make and use

SPA-TYPE AROMATHERAPY FACIAL STEAM

Steaming is a simple concept: just put some water in a pan, bring it to a boil, then drop in essential oils and turn down the heat to low. Drape a towel over your head (to direct the steam to your face, bend over the steam; there will be enough to steam your face for 2 to 3 minutes). You get the benefit of the essential oils on your skin and in your lungs, and the heat will open the pores and sweat the impurities out of them. That's all there is to it!

Make sure you cleanse your skin prior to steaming; we want to work on the grime down in your pores, not the surface dirt. After you're done, pat your skin dry and follow with a moisturizer. Look at the clean and healthy glow you're sporting now!

For relaxation, peace of mind, and cleaning and toning your skin, here is a great blend for steaming. Use all of these essential oils at two drops each, or you can use one or two of them at four drops each:

Bergamot
Clary sage
Geranium
Lavender

MAKE-UP REMOVER FOR FACE AND EYES

This healthy formula will condition skin while it slides make-up right off. Use a cotton ball or tissue and apply to your face and eye area, then gently wipe off (removing make-up and dirt from your skin). After all make-up is removed, rinse your face with water and pat dry.

You Will Need

3 tablespoons coconut oil
3 tablespoons olive oil
1 teaspoon avocado oil

Mix all together. Keep in a bottle and use as needed.

Shelf Life: 4-5 months

Eyelash Conditioner

Mascara dries out eyelashes; these tiny hairs look best when they are not brittle and broken. Natural oils can lubricate and condition eyelashes.

You Will Need

50/50 blend of sweet oil and apricot kernel oil

Mix the sweet oil and apricot kernel oil. Coat your eyelashes lightly with a clean eyelash wand and leave on overnight. Wash off in the morning before applying mascara.

Mother Nature Says ...

For a clear conditioning mascara, brush on Vaseline; it will separate your lashes and make them look longer without coloring them.

Eye Balm (Wrinkle Reducer)

This eye balm will help smooth dry, delicate skin around the eyes. The calendula and chamomile will help soothe irritation. This can double as an eye moisture treatment and will help relieve and heal chapped lips.

You Will Need

1 teaspoon shea butter
1 teaspoon cocoa butter
1 teaspoon canola oil
1 teaspoon olive oil
2 drops calendula extract
1 drop chamomile extract

Melt the shea butter and cocoa butter on low heat. Remove from heat and stir in the remaining ingredients. Continue stirring for 5 minutes, then pour into a bottle.

Shelf Life: 3-5 months

Castile
Soap

Witch Hazel

Tea-tree Oil

Chamomile

CHAPTER 10

Cleansers, Toners, and Scrubs, Oh My!

Toners and astringents are products used to remove any last traces of cleanser or any excess oil and perspiration that is on the skin's surface that may clog its pores. Herbal toners are gentle and do not contain alcohol or acetone, and the herbs and other natural ingredients are chosen for your skin type (i.e. dry or oily).

Cleansers are just that: they cleanse your face of excess sebum, pollution, dirt, etc. and make it ready for the next step (toners). Scrubs are used to exfoliate the skin and remove dead skin layers that are slow to come off (we exfoliate naturally daily, but as you get older, the process happens slower, and old top layers can clog pores and contribute to acne and look rough and wrinkled). So, use a scrub once to twice a week to keep the new, fresh, younger-looking skin at the surface.

Oregano and Tea-tree Toner for Problem Skin

Oregano essential oil is a great antibacterial, and so are tea-tree, nettle, and rosemary. Witch hazel is a natural product that replaces alcohol in this formula. This will perk up and dry up overly oily skin and skin with some acne.

You Will Need

1/2 cup witch hazel
6 drops tea-tree extract
3 drops nettle or rosemary essential oil
6 drops oregano oil or extract

Mix all together and store in the refrigerator. Shake before using.

Shelf Life: 3 to 6 months

Gentle Chamomile and Peppermint Toner for Dry Skin

Chamomile soothes while it tones, and peppermint is a mild toner. With dry skin, you want to just "clarify" the skin, always being cautious not to over-dry it. This is a very gentle toner, which should be followed with a moisturizer.

You Will Need

6 drops chamomile essential oil
6 drops peppermint essential oil
1/4 cup distilled water
1/4 cup witch hazel

Mix all together and store in the refrigerator. Shake before using.

Shelf Life: 3 to 6 months

Mother Nature Says ...

To apply toner, use either a cotton ball or the "splash on" method (although that can be messy).

Rose/Lavender Water and Gin Toner for Normal Skin

This is a balanced toner that will do the trick; it's strong enough to remove all traces of cleanser, but not harsh enough to over-dry your skin. Sounds good enough to drink, but don't! If you don't want the alcohol, substitute witch hazel for the gin.

You Will Need

6 drops rose essential oil
6 drops lavender essential oil
1/4 cup water
1/2 cup gin

Mix all together and store in the refrigerator. Shake before using.

Shelf Life: 3 to 6 months

Herbal, Natural, Gentle Face Cleanser for Everyone

This cleans your face thoroughly and effectively! Just wash your face, rinse clean, and follow with toner and moisturizer.

You Will Need

1/4 cup Liquid Castile Soap
1/8 cup distilled water
3-4 drops chamomile essential oil
1 tablespoon orange or lemon juice

Mix all together and store in the refrigerator.

Shelf Life: 1 to 2 months

PUFFY EYE SOOTHER

Take Mother Nature's two best ingredients for removing red, puffy skin (cucumber and potato), add sage tea and some cold from up north, and you will have an astonishingly effective treatment for swollen, puffy eyes.

You Will Need

1/4 small raw potato, peeled
1/2 of medium-sized cucumber, peeled
2 tablespoons sage infusion (sage tea), cooled

Slice the potato into two chunks and then mash into pieces in a food processor to get them as fine as possible. Use the food processor to puree the peeled cucumber very briefly (do not over-process) and strain the excess juice (although the whole thing will be runny, preserve the more "pulpy" part). Now mix the cucumber, potato, and tea together and pour into an ice cube tray. Freeze. The next time your eyes are puffy, red, and sore, pop one of these ice cubes on them. Leave on for 2 to 3 minutes (or simply "dab" them on, if you are unable to leave them on for that long), rinse your eyelids off, and pat dry. You won't believe your eyes!

Shelf Life: 2 months

CITRUS AND BAKING SODA SCRUB

This is a great scrub for normal to oily skin. It has a slight toning action as it scrubs. You must dehydrate the citrus peels (completely dry them first, then use a food processor or grater to grind it into a fine grainy mix). Aloe and gentle liquid soap work as cleansers, and the citrus peels do the scrubbing.

You Will Need

2 tablespoons ground citrus peels (orange, lemon, or grapefruit)
1/4 cup aloe vera gel
1/2 teaspoon gentle liquid soap (see page 64)
3 drops spearmint essential oil

Mix all together. When applying, use about a teaspoon at a time and add more if needed. Apply to your chin, forehead, and cheeks. Then, wet your fingers with water and gently work in circles around your face (avoiding eye area) for about 1 minute. Rinse off with warm water. You'll love the results… Store in a bottle or container.

Shelf Life: 1 to 2 months

The Good Earth Bath, Beauty & Health Book

Gentle Almond and Oatmeal Scrub

This is a gentle, yet effective, scrub for dry to normal skin that can be used once or twice a week. The ground almonds and oatmeal furnish the scrub, while the aloe vera and gentle liquid soap do the cleansing.

You Will Need

1/4 cup aloe vera gel
1/2 teaspoon gentle liquid soap (see page 64)
2 teaspoons ground almonds
2 teaspoons ground oatmeal

Mix all together. When applying, use about a teaspoon at a time and add more if needed. Apply to your chin, forehead, and cheeks. Then, wet your fingers with water and gently work in circles around your face (avoiding eye area) for about 1 minute. Rinse off with warm water. Store in a bottle or container.

Shelf life: 2 weeks

The Good Earth Bath, Beauty & Health Book

CHAPTER 11

Heavenly Hands and Fabulous Feet

In This Chapter:

Salon-quality Hot Wax Herbal Treatment

Dark Spot/Skin Lightening Bleach

Cuticle and Callous Crème

Citrus/Mint Foot Cooler-Deodorizing Mist

In today's world, it is hard to tell a woman's age by looking at her, because make-up, cosmetic surgery, improved sunscreens for the face, and great moisturizing programs can really make a difference in how a "grandma" looks. So, how do savvy skin care professionals know where to look to guess a client's real age? They check the backs of the hands and/or feet while giving a treatment. These hardworking parts of our bodies often get the worst of climate changes and exposure—and the least "beauty care." Here are some spa-quality formulas, using Mother Nature's best, to help keep your hands and feet healthy and young looking.

SALON-QUALITY HOT WAX HERBAL TREATMENT

Have you ever gone for a paraffin dip at a professional spa? It leaves your hands feeling incredibly moisturized. The oil melts right into the wax and gives it a "moisturizing" effect. This is how it works: The beeswax, as it dries on your skin, tightens and forces the moisturizing oil into your skin. The warmth of the wax softens the skin and opens the pores, and the oils are temporarily "trapped" in your skin, because the coating of beeswax does not allow evaporation to occur. This creates a very quick "deep therapy" treatment for either the hands or feet that leaves them baby soft for a good period of time. Both essential oils in this formula have smoothing, soothing qualities.

If you have stiff, sore hands and/or feet, substitute the lavender and chamomile for 5 drops wintergreen, 3 drops peppermint, and 2 drops camphor (for analgesic relief). Heat from the wax will give you a deep heat-analgesic treat.

In order to keep a steady heat, put this formula in a crock pot **and use extreme caution when dipping your hand or foot into the wax.** The wax should be cool enough to use when a crust has formed over the top. If you cannot fit your hand or foot in the crock pot, pour the wax treatment into a pan deep and wide enough to fit them in; use immediately.

You Will Need

1 cup quality beeswax (block or chips)
10 tablespoon sweet almond oil
8 tablespoon virgin olive oil
5 drops lavender essential oil
3 drops chamomile essential oil

Melt the beeswax in the crock pot (you must use low heat; do not turn on medium or high because wax can cause a fire if it gets too hot). When it is melted, add all of the oils and stir. You will want to put the wax in a pan large enough to hold one hand (or foot) at a time. Make sure the wax is very warm but not too hot; you do not want to burn yourself! Use a candy thermometer to test if you are unsure (a temperature of 91 to 98 degrees is perfect). Dip one hand in one at a time, sit back, relax and enjoy. Wait about 7 to 10 minutes until the wax is set up. Peel off.

You can reuse the wax several times, so this is a real environmental product! The formula will last up to a year, but if it gets too dry, or loses its aroma, just add a little more oil. This is a great product for a "beauty slumber party" with the girls, and the formula can be doubled or tripled to make more! Store in a container.

Shelf Life: Up to 1 year

DARK SPOT/SKIN LIGHTENING BLEACH

Lemon juice and oil of orange both work as mild skin bleaches. The baking soda helps "activate" the process, the water is to dilute it into a paste, and milk was used in Cleopatra's time to whiten (I'm not sure it actually did much of that, but I couldn't resist adding it here!) and will serve here to help soften and soothe the skin during the "bleaching" process.

1/2 lemon, squeezed and strained
1 tablespoon baking soda
1 tablespoon powdered milk
2 drops orange essential oil
Water

Mix the first four ingredients together. Add water, a very small amount at a time while mixing, until you get a very soft paste. Apply to the skin on dark, uneven areas or on age spots (this can be used on the face for freckles, too). Leave on for 5 minutes, then wash off and apply moisturizer.

Shelf Life: None; make and use

Mother Nature Says ...

HELPFUL HINT FOR HANDS AND FEET. SO MANY PEOPLE CAREFULLY RUB SUNSCREEN ON THEIR FACES AND BODIES, BUT TOTALLY IGNORE THE BACK OF THE HAND. THIS IS AN AREA THAT GETS SOME OF THE HEAVIEST SUN EXPOSURE AND THE LEAST CARE. KEEP HANDS LOOKING YOUNG BY PROTECTING THEM WITH "EXTRA" SUNSCREEN, OR AS YOUNG AS YOU MAY APPEAR, YOU MAY NOT FOOL THE SAVVY LOOKER! IN THE SUMMER, IF YOU ARE A BAREFOOT GAL, CONSIDER USING EXTRA SUNSCREEN ON THE TOPS OF YOUR FEET, TOO.

CUTICLE AND CALLOUS CRÈME

The little bit of natural Vitamin E occurring in the wheat germ oil will help its shelf life. This is a formula that combines "super rich" oils for those extra dry areas that need special conditioning. (I use this in the winter on my knees, elbows, and heels, and totally avoid those dry, chapped "winter dried" blues.)

5 tablespoons cocoa butter
1 teaspoon wheatgerm oil
3 tablespoons avocado oil
3 drops rosemary essential oil

Heat cocoa butter until just melted. Stir in other ingredients until cooled (about 5 minutes), which is important to blend oils. Rub into cuticles and calluses for super softening.

Shelf life: About 2 to 3 months

CITRUS/MINT FOOT COOLER-DEODORIZING MIST

Whew, a long name, but it does it all. Wintergreen and peppermint will deodorize and work against bacteria, as does the witch hazel, plus it helps give a cooling feeling. The lemon and grapefruit "freshen" and help with the process too… This is my favorite when I have been "speed walking" on a hot day. It is a great gift for athletes because it helps cool down sore leg muscles after running marathons—and the blast of herbs and citrus help give them a "pick-up refresher" to help them combat their fatigue. I keep mine in the refrigerator because it adds to the cooling sensation the ingredients give and helps prolong the shelf life.

1/4 cup distilled water
1/4 cup witch hazel
3 drops lemon fragrance oil
3 drops grapefruit fragrance oil
2 drops wintergreen essential oil
2 drops peppermint essential oil

Mix all together. Pour into sportier and store in the refrigerator. Shake well before using.

Shelf Life: Approx. 2 to 3 weeks

The Good Earth Bath, Beauty & Health Book

Color and Shine for Your Lips

In This Chapter:

Basic Lip Gloss Formula

Flavored Lip Gloss

Soft Color Lip Gloss

Herbal Flavored Lip Balm

In early times, women would pinch their cheeks and bite their lips to give them color... Well, that may be a "natural side-effect" of a certain action, but it's not my idea of a good time! Here are some natural lip products that you can make at home to give yourself a treat as well as gifts. The great thing is that these do not need preservatives to have a good shelf life. All of these formulas will last several months when kept in a closed pot. My test group says these are the most fun to make and give as gifts—not to mention how much fun you can have playing with different flavors and formula consistency.

BASIC LIP GLOSS FORMULA

This is a "mostly" natural formula; our only deviation is with the petroleum jelly, but it is really hard to find anything in nature that will give the cosmetic high-gloss finish it does. Also, petroleum jelly plays a good role here in that it helps seal the lips against dehydration, while the beeswax gives the formula "body," and the aloe vera and apricot kernel condition your lips, as well as help with the "glide." This formula can be flavored (see the next column).

You Will Need

1 teaspoon beeswax
1 teaspoon petroleum jelly
1/2 teaspoon aloe vera gel
1/2 teaspoon apricot kernel oil

Melt the beeswax, then remove from heat and add the petroleum jelly and aloe vera gel right away. Stir for 1 to 2 minutes until completely dissolved. Add the apricot kernel oil and stir for another minute. Pour into pots and use over lipstick or alone for a "movie star" shine. Store in a cool, dry place.

Shelf Life: 6+ months

Mother Nature Says ...

IF YOU ADD A LITTLE MORE PETROLEUM JELLY AND COLOR TO THE BASIC LIP GLOSS FORMULA, YOU CAN MAKE A GLIDE-ON GLOSSY BLUSHER.

FLAVORED LIP GLOSS

Add flavor at the same time as the apricot kernel oil to the Basic Lip Gloss Formula. The basic rules are not to add more than three drops of flavoring and to use flavoring purchased at a grocery or cake decorating store.

SOFT COLOR LIP GLOSS

You can also add color to your lip gloss (along with a flavor). Commercial colorants that are safe for cosmetic use are hard to find at consumer stores. Look for non-toxic crayons for children (the kind that are labeled non-toxic are made with mild colorants with the assumption that children might put them in their mouths). Shave the colored crayon (reds work the best) and melt about 1/4 teaspoon into the lip gloss formula, and you will have a lightly colored lip gloss that will help "color" your lips.

Your lips are conditioned, shiny, colored, and flavored. You look great, Cinderella, whether you smile or pout!

Mother Nature Says ...

IT IS GREAT FUN TO MIX YOUR OWN SPECIAL LIP GLOSS FLAVORS! BY MIXING CRANBERRY AND LEMON, YOU WILL GET BUBBLEGUM, OR HOW ABOUT THOSE CRAZY KIDS' BEVERAGE FLAVORS, LIKE STRAWBERRY/BANANA, CHERRY/VANILLA, CHOCOLATE/PEPPERMINT, OR...

HERBAL FLAVORED LIP BALM

How fun! You can make this in a range of flavors. This formula will assist with hydrating dry chapped lips.

You Will Need

1 teaspoon beeswax
3-1/2 teaspoons sweet almond oil
1/2 teaspoon aloe vera gel
6 drops of your favorite herbal flavoring (or other flavoring), including peppermint, spearmint, lemon, orange, cinnamon, strawberry, etc.

Melt the beeswax and oil together in a small pan over low heat. Remove from heat and add the aloe vera gel, stirring for about 5 minutes. As the mixture cools, add the flavoring (you can combine more than one flavoring in the six drops). Put in little plastic lip balm jars or other small containers.

Shelf Life: 6+ months

Mother Nature Says ...

WITH ANY OF THESE LIP FORMULAS, YOU CAN ADJUST THE AMOUNT OF "SLIDE AND GLOSS." IF YOU WANT THE FORMULA GLOSSIER OR THINNER SO IT SLIDES EASIER, SIMPLY INCREASE THE AMOUNT OF APRICOT KERNEL OR SWEET ALMOND OIL. IF YOU THINK THE MIXTURE IS TOO "LOOSE" OR GLOSSY, JUST INCREASE THE AMOUNT OF BEESWAX IN YOUR NEXT BATCH.

The Good Earth Bath, Beauty & Health Book

CHAPTER 13

Essential Perfume Oils, Solids, and Sprays

In This Chapter:

Blending Fragrances

Perfume Oil

Eau de Toilette Perfume

Perfume Balm

After Bath Splash: Essential Oil or Perfume Spray

Exotic Herbal Dusting Powder

Making your own perfume blends and types is really fun. You can use these various forms of perfume distribution methods for making a "single note" or "mixed note" aromatherapy product. For hints on which essential oils to use for various responses, see page 16 for some botanicals and their aromatherapy responses. Then, simply add the number of drops indicated in the formula when "fragrance oil" is mentioned.

These formulas can be made with either pure essential oils or synthetic reproductions, but they must be "essential oil grade" fragrances in strength. Do not be tempted to sub-

stitute cologne or perfume when the formula calls for "fragrance oil" because the product is too diluted to work. You will be using essential oil or synthetic fragrance oil concentrates to make into perfume oil, perfumes, and sprays for your use.

After you have made your product, be sure to store it in a cool, dark place, because fragrances and essential oils are venerable to light and heat.

First, I will teach you a little about fragrance blending in this chapter so that you can have fun working as your own personal "perfumer."

Blending Fragrances (or Essential Oils)

A good perfumer will always try to balance the "notes" or "character" of aromas to create a balanced bouquet. Just like a fine wine balances several different types of flavors in harmony on your tongue, for a taste "experience," so do aromas have sympathetic characters that create a "rounding" to the olfactory response. A well-balanced, interesting blend can delight your tongue and give you pleasurable associations with certain foods. In the same sense, a well-balanced and interesting blend of fragrances can evoke a pleasant mood or memory, as well as some physical responses. Most single aromas have a character that is referred to as a "note" (just like a note in music, they all fall in a range from high to low notes by their smell character). These notes are known as High Notes, Mid Notes, and Low Notes. It takes a little while to develop this identification by your sense of smell, and trying to explain this by writing to you and not by example is quite a challenge, but let's try...

I will give you an example from each so that you get the idea. I really do not like generalities in an exacting science, but perfuming is a complicated science, and I will give you some to get you started.

High Notes are sharp and strong. They are usually floral and carry a long-lasting punch. A morning tea rose that is picked early in its bloom and early in the day is very sweet and is usually a High Note (although a rose picked later from a full or late bloom can sometimes round to a Mid Note).

Mid Notes are solid, pleasurable smells that will seem to be medium in strength and are "mellow" to smell. They are great "blending" notes. My favorite Mid Note used to soften and blend fragrances together is vanilla.

Low Notes are usually dark, musky, or deeply spicy in their descriptions. Musk or patchouli are usually in this range.

Okay, now you have some information on notes. When you start to put together a blend, there are a few basic principles to know. Seldom does any blend of two or more aromas smell good when put together in equal proportions. This is because they usually will compete too much, and your olfactory response will become confused. You really need to pick a main theme, one note that will dominate the blend. Even though a person's nose may not be able to pick out the main note when smelling the blend, the nose seems to demand a main note. Only experienced perfumers can pull off a balanced blend of dominate aromas mixed together. Here are the basics:

1. Pick your main aroma.

2. As a beginner, do not try to blend more than two or three aromas together for best results.

3. When you smell the main aroma, decide if it is a High, Mid, or Low Note. Then, blend one or two others with it.

Here is a natural essential oil formula that is a slight aphrodisiac and romantic blend. It is a simple three-blend perfume that is also a synergistic essential oil compound (this is where the two concepts, aromatherapy and perfumery, overlap). And it is ready to make into a perfume oil, solid, or spray.

You Will Need

5 drops early blooming rose (High Note, main aroma choice)

2 drops vanilla (Mid Note, great for mellowing out the High Note and softening the aroma)

1 drop allspice (Low Note, gives spicy, exotic note and lends interest to blend that is softened by the vanilla)

When you are blending, even one drop of essence or aroma in a whole big bottle of another aroma will make a big difference in the smell, which brings us to:

4. Never mix together the aromas before you first try them out on paper strips. This process will save you a lot of money because you won't loose much of your essential/fragrance oil when trying your initial ideas.

Using Paper Strips

Use white, lightweight construction paper or any other white paper that has some substance to it (a little fibrous texture). Most white papers will work except for extremely flimsy paper or paper that has any kind of gloss on it. Cut the paper into strips, approximately 1/8-inch wide and 2-1/2 inches long. You will probably need to cut a dozen or so for your first attempt at blending.

Line up the essential oil vials (or fragrance oil vials) that you have chosen to use for your first blend. Using one strip only per vial, dip a paper strip into the vial, just enough to put a very small amount of "aroma" on the tip of the paper. Bring it out of the bottle and repeat the process with new papers and one or two other aromas you want in the blend. Be careful not to touch these to each other or you will lose the "purity" of the experiment. Now, hold each of the papers together in one hand, with them touching at the base, not at the fragranced end. Adjust the heights of these strips so that your Main Note fragrance is the tallest, and continue to make them shorter based on how you think you want to use them.

Now, wave all three pieces of paper back and forth under your nose and you will get an idea of how they will smell when mixed together. Try rearranging them at different heights and smell again. You have used very little of your precious oils and have an idea of what you will be creating.

When you are pleased, go ahead and mix the oils together and get ready to use your new blends whether for aromatherapy or just as perfume, into the following products.

PERFUME OIL

Add equal amounts of a great carrier oil like jojoba oil with your single note essential or your newly created blend. You now have a mix that is still very strong but will be a grade suitable for use on the skin as a perfume. Dab behind your ears, wrists, and other "pulse" points. Store in a dark glass vial.

Shelf Life: 6 to 12 months

EAU DE TOILETTE PERFUME

Most perfumes are fragrance in alcohol and are made with sp40 alcohol. You cannot buy that over the counter, so I have substituted "low smell" alcohols here to do the trick.

You Will Need

1/4 cup 90-proof vodka or everclear
2 tablespoons essential oil or blended oil

Blend together and put in a pretty bottle.

Shelf Life: 6 to 10 months

Mother Nature Says ...

KEEP RECORDS AS TO WHAT YOU DID SO YOU CAN RECREATE A BLEND LATER. ALSO, BE PREPARED THAT SOMETIMES YOUR IDEAS WILL TURN OUT WONDERFULLY, AND SOMETIMES THEY WON'T!

Perfume Balm

This is not only a perfume but also a salve for areas that are rough. We use beeswax here because it is natural and sets up to a solid. Beeswax is often used as the natural solid base for lip balms, salves, and any other base that you might want a solid, coating/moisturizing base. The problem with beeswax in its solid state is that it is not soft enough to dispense. It is more of a "coating agent" than a real moisturizing agent, so that is why we add natural oils. Jojoba is in this formula to add a little natural preservative, as well as to help with the softening of the beeswax and the moisturizing of the skin. Jojoba and apricot kernel will both help solubulize the essential/fragrance oil into the wax but they will both add moisturizing for the skin and do the trick for loosening the beeswax to help it dispense easily from the decorative tin to your skin.

This is really like a solid perfume, but has a lot of moisturizing qualities. Use on your knees and elbows, or a little on your pulse points, to make you fragrant and soft. After you have made your first batch, if you want your end product firmer, increase the beeswax a little, and if you want it softer, increase the apricot kernel oil a little.

You Will Need

1/4 cup beeswax
4 tablespoons jojoba oil
1 tablespoon essential/fragrance oil (or mix; see page 96 on blending)
1/4 cup apricot kernel oil

Heat and melt the beeswax in a double boiler on medium heat (do not leave unattended). As soon as it is melted, remove from heat, quickly mix the oils and essential/fragrance oils together, and then add to the beeswax, stirring for about 1 minute. Pour into decorative tins or small glass or plastic jars (if you use plastic, make sure that they can stand the heat of the initial pour) and let set up overnight.

Shelf Life: 6 to 12 months

Mother Nature Says ...

THE GREAT THING ABOUT THIS FORMULA IS, IF THE SHELF LIFE EXPIRES AND YOUR FRAGRANCE WANES, JUST REMELT, ADJUST THE FORMULA (IF NEEDED) TO MAKE IT SOFTER OR FIRMER, AND RE-ADD THE ESSENTIAL OR FRAGRANCE OIL.

After Bath Splash: Essential Oil or Perfume Spray

This is a great way to "mist" on either your favorite relaxing blend for aromatherapy purposes or just to make a great little perfume "freshener" from the perfuming skills I taught you earlier in this chapter.

You Will Need

1/8 cup 90-proof vodka
1/8 cup distilled water
8-10 drops essential or fragrance oil

Dissolve the essential oil in the alcohol first and let sit for about an hour to "mature." Slowly add the water portion to the alcohol/fragrance blend and shake gently. Pour into a decorative bottle (a dark bottle will help preserve the product longer; remember that essentials and fragrances don't like high-light and high-heat environments) and store in the refrigerator. Shake before using.

Shelf Life: Approx. 4 to 6 months

Mother Nature Says ...

HERE ARE SOME PULSE POINTS AND OTHER POPULAR PLACES TO PUT FRAGRANCES AND ESSENTIAL OILS:

- BEHIND KNEES
- INSIDE OF ELBOWS
- BASE OF THROAT
- BETWEEN BREASTS
- TEMPLES
- BEHIND EARS

Exotic Herbal Dusting Powder

This very fine powder is great for dusting on anytime to cool and smooth your skin. Try on your sheets, in your shoes, over your deodorant to "set it," or…

Mixed essential oils of frankincense, ylang-ylang, rose, and chamomile mixed as follows:
4 drops frankincense
1 drop ylang-ylang
1 drop rose
1 drop chamomile
1/2 cup arrowroot powder
1/2 cup rice flour

Using a hand sieve, sift the powder and flour together. Then, drop one drop of oil at a time on the powder mix and resift the whole blend. You must do this six times, once for each drop you add to the mix. It takes a lot of sifting to force the oils into the flour! Put in a large tin and let the whole mixture sit and absorb for about one week. Finally, put in decorative tins with a puff or in a cheese shaker.

Shelf Life: 6+ months

The Good Earth Bath, Beauty & Health Book

Herbal Remedy and Toiletry Gifts: Ideas and How to Package Your Creations With Love

In This Chapter:

Home Spa Set

TLC Basket

Lovers Package

9-5 Basket

Campers Delight

Throughout the book, I have mentioned decorative jars, containers, and tins. Now is the time to start watching for unusual packaging. Look at antiques stores, garage sales, and specialty stores for antique- and old fashioned-looking items. Specialty stores now have interesting glass and plastic bottles, as well as decorative tins. Check specialty kitchenware and gourmet shops, too (look for a unique cheese shaker for your powder or vinegar carafe for your massage oil). Your favorite craft store is full of unique items to help you create and decorate your creations. Always be on the look-out for cleaver items you can use.

THE GARNISH

Dried herb stems, unusual ribbon, lace strips, silk or dried flowers, and raffia are just a few examples of "garnish" for your gifts. These will be tied on to make bows, secure hang-tags, or decorate a gift basket or container. Remember the "finish" of your gift helps represent the quality and loving care you took making the homemade products inside.

Labels can be homemade with love. My favorite are hang-tags, which are really small place cards folded in half and with a hole in the upper corner. This makes a "mini-card" that you can write a special message in, along with instructions for use and storage. You can then run a ribbon, piece of raffia, or a bit of lace through the hole and tie it onto the bottle, jar, bag, or basket. You can also make interesting "stick on" labels using your computer and mailing labels, or use your paper cutting skills to hand cut and decorate a flat tied-on label. Rubber stamps can be fun to use to create labels, too!

What will you put your gift ideas in for presentation? Most people would say "baskets," and this is a good idea, but also consider decorative gift bags, large see-through vinyl or plastic bags, cute buckets, netting bags, fabric cosmetic travel bags, a large tin bucket, or just "unique packaging" that is inventive and fun. Once you get started thinking about this, you will find packaging everywhere you look. Here are some examples of fun and unique packaging (see pages 106-108 for gift themes).

- Plastic trick or treat bucket with the TLC set.
- Kid's tin lunch pail with the 9-5 gift set (does your friend have a favorite movie or cartoon character?).
- Get well soon basket in one of those cheery decorative bags with bright colors and lots of tissue.
- Two Lovers' Package items taped to the front of a romance novel and then tied up with a big bow.

Use decorative strips of netting, special plastic decorative wrap, or just good old plastic wrap to finish the basket. Cut long strips at least three times longer than your gift item. Lay out the wrap in a large cross as shown.

Pull up around the gift items, gather evenly, and tie at the top with ribbon or trim as needed.

Home Spa Set

Gather some nail polish and remover, nail files, and washcloths and towels, and you and your friends are all set for a night of relaxing, pampering, and beautifying that will make Mother Nature proud!

🌿 Tranquility Relaxing Oil, page 53

🌿 Herbal/Botanical Protein Dry Hair Deep Conditioner, page 67

🌿 Cuticle and Callous Crème, page 88

🌿 Body Butter Crème for Dry Skin, page 70

🌿 Essential oils for facial steam, page 76

🌿 Gentle Chamomile and Peppermint Toner, page 80

🌿 Gentle Almond Oatmeal Scrub, page 83

🌿 The ingredients and instructions for one of the facial masks, pages 74-76

TLC Basket (Flu Season)

When you give this gift to a sick loved-one or friend, he or she will feel pampered and cared for, knowing how much you care by taking the time to prepare this with your own hands. Also include a package of tissues and either some rolled up magazines or a good book.

🌿 Lemon and Honey Drops, page 35

🌿 Expectorant Cough Syrup, page 36

🌿 Headache Tea Formula, page 34

🌿 Night-time Cold Formula, page 37

LOVERS' PACKAGE

I like to give this package at bridal showers, but you could also give it to your spouse at Christmas time with a few IOUs… and also add a few candles, chocolates for your pillows, a bottle of wine, two glasses, and a romantic music CD. This special, thoughtful gift will be remembered for months.

- Super Moisturizing Massage Oil, page 51
- Oil Exotique, page 53
- Scented Gentle Bubble Bath, page 42
- Herbal Bath Salts, page 45

9-5 BASKET

This is a great gift for Mother's Day, Secretaries Day, or for your best friend to show her you care. Put in a book to read in the bath and maybe some of her favorite music, along with a candle.

- Fizzy Bath Crystals ("Fizzy Shapes"), page 46, or Bath Butter, page 44
- Cuticle Crème, page 88
- Minty Cleansing Cold Crème, page 71
- Puffy Eye Soother, page 82 (write the instructions for use on a pretty piece of paper wrapped with a ribbon)
- Citrus/Mint Foot Cooler-Deodorizing Mist, page 89
- Flavored Lip Gloss, page 92

CAMPER'S DELIGHT

This is a great gift for campers or people who spend a lot of time outdoors. Put this in a medium-sized utility pail or plastic wash bin; either will be handy at the campsite. Stick in a fire starter, some candles in tins or flashlights, and a blanket and they are all set! Sometimes, I tuck in a roll of toilet paper, too; it takes up lots of space in the basket, but it always seems to come in handy.

❧ Bug Bite Soother, page 32
❧ Lip Balm, page 93
❧ Sweet Oil, page 32
❧ Antiseptic Wound Wash, page 38
❧ Quick Sunburn Calmer, page 39

Christmas and birthdays are occasions when very personal gifts can be tailored to your friend and loved one. Just look through this book for ideas or follow one of the basket examples given.

In this busy world, homemade gifts are really still the best way to show that you care enough to take the time to hand-make a care item just for your loved one or friend. This is just a start, a suggestion of some themes that I have done or thought about doing, and I am sure you will think of many more.

Finding Natural Ingredients

I found all of the ingredients used in this book in one of the following locations: health food store, grocery store, pharmacies, garden shops, perfumers, hardware stores, liquor stores, and craft stores. You can look for other sources in the Yellow Pages under these headings: botanicals, herbs, spices, oils, and health foods. You may even be able to find these ingredients by researching on the Internet or from mail-order companies.

I did not list a lot of the more common ingredients because they really need no explanation. Here are some special hints to keep in mind:

- Antiseptic: A germ killer or ingredient that helps sterilize the skin.
- Analgesic: An ingredient or blend that helps kill pain.
- Essential oils: You can find these at health food stores, some gift and craft stores, and perfumers.
- Herbs: Fresh or dried herbs can be found at garden centers, health food stores, grocery stores, and herb shops.
- Oils as carriers, for massage or bath: All of the oils you purchase should say "cold pressed" or "cold pressed, virgin oil" on them. Cold pressed oils maintain their vitamin content and are better for your skin. These are available at most health food stores.

Aloe vera gel: From the aloe plant; the leaves produce a light gel. Most gels are thickened (it is a liquid when it comes directly from the plant). Aloe is soothing for sunburns or minor skin irritations and is also a very mild astringent. If you have trouble finding it, you can buy a clear aloe after-sun cooler and use that as a base, or you can grow an aloe plant at home (just slice and squeeze the aloe from the leaves and stem).

Apricot kernel oil: This oil is derived from the apricot kernel. This is my favorite "light" oil and carrier oil mixed with a little jojoba. Apricot kernel oil is an emollient, which is used for softening the skin.

Arrowroot powder: A bland, gentle powder (starch) that is similar to cornstarch but is usually much finer. It has great drying abilities.

Avocado oil: Oil from an avocado's pulp is very heavy and nourishing to the skin (although it has a short shelf life).

Beeswax: A natural wax that is a by-product of bees. It is used both in toiletries and cosmetics, as well as candlemaking.

Bicarbonate of soda (baking soda): Baking soda is a natural odor eater and is used in many products. It has the ability to "draw out" the infection and burn of an insect sting and is soothing to the skin. It also acts as a natural deodorizer.

Borax (sodium borate): A white mineral powder from the desert. It is used as a water softener or emulsifier and sometimes as a toner in cosmetics.

Camphor oil: This is a topical antiseptic and analgesic derived from either the camphor tree (from the wood) or it is synthetically produced.

Castile soap, liquid: A gentle olive oil soap that was first made and sold in Castile, Spain (most of it is no longer made there but the name is still used).

Chamomile oil or herb: Made from chamomile flowers, this is a soothing ingredient that is also a mild astringent and mild anti-inflammatory. When ingested, it can also be calming.

Chloroform, liquid: The green color in a lot of plants and leafy vegetables, chloroform is a natural cleanser both inside and out and works as a mild astringent and toner.

Citric acid: Fruit acid that can adjust pH as well as have an antioxidant and toning effect.

Cocoa butter: This is derived from the seeds of the cacao tree and is a fat that is separated out during the process of making cocoa. Cocoa butter is a rich, hard oil that is also used to make candy—it smells, but doesn't taste, like chocolate. This butter is an emollient and softens and smooths the skin.

Coconut oil: The Hawaiians have sworn by this one for years! A great moisturizer and emollient, coconut oil is also solid at room temperature. Other great Hawaiian oils are macadamia nut oil and kukui nut oil, which are also emollients.

French Clay: Sometimes known as green clay, this is widely used for cosmetic purposes. It works by drawing out the impurities from the skin and is full of natural minerals.

Glycerin: This can come from animals or vegetables. Glycerin is a terrific moisturizer that has the ability to attract moisture in the air and bring it to the skin. I recommend vegetable glycerin for a couple of reasons. First, vegetable glycerin is easier for your skin to absorb, and second, no animal needs to be harmed.

Jojoba oil: This is an expensive oil, but well worth it. It contains a small amount of natural Vitamin E, which helps preserve it longer than most oils. It is similar to the oil our own skin produces.

Kava kava: A Pacific Island treasure. This botanical has long been used by natives as a soothing tranquilizer to combat anxiety. The compounds known as kavalactones, or kavapyrones, are the active elements in this botanical.

Nettle: Also known as stinging nettle or common nettle, this soothes and warms the skin and acts as a natural, mild antiseptic. It is often used in compresses to calm irritations and pain.

Olive oil, virgin: An emollient that is a favorite in Spain. Good for you inside and out, it is often used in skin care and hair formulas. It is a heavy oil and often needs to be combined with a lighter oil.

Orris root powder: This comes from the root of the iris flower. The rhizome, which is dried and then powdered or cut into small pieces, is used as a "fixative" in home potpourri or sachet making (but not for use on the skin).

Pectin: This is most commonly sold as a powder; it is a natural carbohydrate that is the base for most edible jellies.

Salt: From the sea or the Great Salt Lake. Used to tone the skin and as an exfoliant.

Shea butter: It is used in a lot of the commercial body butters. Shea butter comes from the Shea tree in Africa, where every part of the tree is used. Shea is an emollient. It is solid at room temperature but melts easily and can be mixed with small amounts of natural oils.

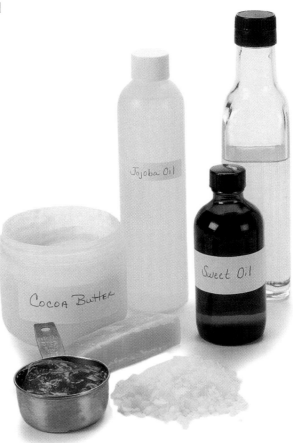

Sweet almond oil: An emollient. This moisturizer is a mid-weight oil, which removes eye makeup and is a great all-purpose body oil from almonds.

Sweet oil: The very purest form of olive oil. If you cannot find it, ask your pharmacist.

Tea-tree oil or extract: From the Melaleuca tree in Australia, this substance is a natural antibacterial, antifungal, and antiseptic. You will find it in many natural deodorizers and antiseptic formulas on the market. The oil is not as strong as the extract (I prefer the extract, but it is hard to find).

Vetiver: A tall, upright grass that grows in clumps. The roots are sometimes used in perfume manufacture and were used by native peoples as an insect repellent. It is known in the tropics as Khus-Khus.

Wheatgerm oil: This is a very heavy emollient oil. It also has some natural Vitamin E to help preserve it, but it needs to be blended with lighter oils or it is too thick for body use. If used alone, it can have a "sticky" feel, but when mixed with other oils, it loses that feel completely.

Witch hazel: The bark and leaves of the witch hazel bush are used a natural antiseptic or astringent. This is a great replacement item for alcohol in toners and fresheners.

Formula Index